MARK ANTONY

Pat Southern

MARK ANTONY

Pat Southern

TEMPUS

For a modern Tony, who listens,
buys the coffees and carries the books.

First published 1998

Published by:
Tempus Publishing Limited
The Mill, Brimscombe Port
Stroud, Gloucestershire, GL5 2QG

Typesetting and origination by Tempus Publishing Ltd.
Printed and bound in Great Britain.

British Library Cataloguing in Publication Data.
A catalogue record for this book is available from the British Library.

ISBN 07524 1406 2

Contents

Acknowledgements

This book owes its origin to the persistence and encouragement of Peter Kemmis Betty, who believed that I could do it, but its true origins go back much further, to the days of Latin lessons at school, reading Caesar's *Gallic Wars*, combined with the discovery of second hand bookshops, libraries, and epic films in glorious Technicolour. For the sake of dramatic cohesion, film-makers may not always have adhered to the strict truth, but that never mattered. What they did was to foster and nourish an interest that was already there, and to inspire a lifelong quest to find out where it all came from. It has been a pleasure to research the subject of Antony's life, and to try to discern the real man behind the violent abuse of Cicero, the propaganda of Octavian and the possible distortions of the later sources. Despite efforts to obliterate Antony, he still emerges as a vivid personality, imperfect, sometimes impetuous, misunderstood, but infinitely more fun to be with than many of his contemporaries. It is very difficult to remain impartial when writing about Antony.

I owe a perennial debt to Graeme Stobbs for drawing the maps and plans, and to Karen Dixon for lending photos. I am grateful to the following museums and agencies for supplying photographs: British Museum, London; Capitoline Museum, Rome; Cherchel Museum, Algeria, courtesy Agence Nationale d'Archéologie et de Protection des Sites et Monuments Historiques, Algiers; National Trust Photographic Library; Musée Archéologique, Narbonne; Vatican Museums, Vatican City; Wellington Museum, London, courtesy Victoria and Albert Museum.

The illustrations

The front-cover illustration of Mark Antony is reproduced by courtesy of the Musées de Narbonne

1 A mis-spent youth

It is a strange fact that, although Mark Antony is such a well-known figure, even to those who are not specialists in Roman history, no-one knows precisely when he was born. Three dates have been suggested, 86, 83 and 81 BC. Most modern scholars opt for the middle date of 83. Even the ancient authors could not agree on this topic, since they were not sure of his age at death, when he committed suicide in 30 BC. We are variously informed that he was 56 years old or possibly only 51, and at this distance in time there is no way of establishing the truth. Whatever the precise year, Antony's birthday was 14 January. After his defeat at the battle of Actium, this day was declared *nefastus* by a compliant Senate acting on the orders of Octavian, the victor of the battle. *Nefastus* means unholy, or at best unlucky, and on such days no public business could be transacted. It was all part of the process of having Antony's memory damned forever (in Latin, *damnatio memoriae*). Octavian was thorough on this point. He had little to fear from Antony after the battle of Actium, and nothing at all to fear after the fall of Alexandria and the suicide of Antony in the following year. There remained the problem of self-justification, however, which entailed the further blackening of Antony's name in order to convince the Romans of the great danger that would have faced the state if the hero Octavian had neglected to engage the enemy in combat to the death. Even when Octavian had achieved virtual sole rule in 27 and had been transformed into Augustus, he would not yield and reverse the process, restoring Antony's memory. It was left to Caligula, Antony's great-grandson, to do that.

Despite attempts to wipe him from the record, Antony's memory lives on, preserved through the ages via the ancient biographers and historians, whose work was duplicated by assiduous monkish copyists; the image of Antony was glorified by Shakespeare's tragedies, and perpetuated for the modern world in novels, plays and films. Mark Antony can be viewed from several angles as the roisterous youth, the bluff soldier, Caesar's lieutenant, the brutal slayer of Cicero, Cleopatra's paramour, Octavian's enemy. He can be seen as a heroic loser fighting for a lost cause, or a pathetic failure who threw everything away for the sake of a woman. Much of what we think of Antony has been moulded for us by Octavian's presentation of him to the Roman public. Remaining aloof from Rome from 43 onwards, Antony had no voice in the political developments in the city, nor did his supporters really gain the political upper hand, except on odd occasions, and for minor matters. Following his death, his partisans were silenced or seduced. After the turmoil of the civil wars it was worth sacrificing his memory for the sake of peace, so he found few champions to speak up for him, but his descendants were not victimized because of their connections with him; indeed most of them were elevated to high rank. As part of a political alliance Antony had married Octavian's elder sister, Octavia, by whom he had two daughters, the younger of whom was the great lady Antonia, the mother of Germanicus and Claudius. The later descendants were not so worthy. Caligula was Antony's great-grandson, and Nero was descended from Antony via both his parents; his father Gnaeus Domitius Ahenobarbus was Antony's grandson; his mother Agrippina was Antony's great-grandaughter. Neither Caligula nor Nero proved any great credit to Antony's memory, both of them suffering the same fate after death of *damnatio memoriae.*

Antony's origins did not presage fame or fortune, nor even a mildly distinguished career. His family was neither wealthy nor important. His grandfather, also called Marcus Antonius as were all the first-born sons in the family, was the first to reach the consulship in 99. He had risen to prominence as an orator and lawyer. Skill in these professions was a great asset in ancient Rome, where the path to fame and glory often began in the law courts. From 113 to 112 Marcus Antonius was in Cilicia, combatting the ever-present menace of the pirates who were based there. After his consulship he was one of the censors in 97; as with the consulship there were always two censors, who were responsible for taking the five yearly census and registering the people in their voting tribes. They were also responsible for overseeing public morals and could eject men from the Senate if they were deemed unsuitable. The censorship was a prestigious office; not many senators achieved such high status. Ten years after his censorship, Marcus Antonius was killed in the proscriptions of 87, having fallen into the wrong camp during the struggle between Marius and Sulla.

The background to this struggle requires brief explanation because it had great bearing upon the careers of Gnaeus Pompey and Gaius Julius Caesar, and then Antony and Octavian. Gaius Marius was the famous general who had saved Rome from the invasions of the Celtic peoples who swept down from the north in the late second century BC. Marius was a parvenu, not politically experienced, but as a general he was supreme, taking the field year after year in the war against the Celts. He was elected to the consulship six times, which was both unprecedented and not strictly constitutional, but in times of danger the will of the people prevailed. When the external threats were eradicated, there was internal strife, resulting in the Social War which broke out in 90. Rome's Italian allies went to war to gain enfranchisement and proper integration in the Roman world. Rome was churlish at first, perfectly willing to sacrifice Italians for her own protection but then unwilling to confer on them the benefits of Roman citizenship. Lucius Cornelius Sulla was an impoverished aristocrat who fought against the Italian rebels, and gained the consulship in 88. By then most of the internal fighting was over, and citizenship was granted to the Italians who had remained loyal. The civil war was eclipsed because a new danger was looming. King Mithridates of Pontus had invaded territories in Asia, which Rome claimed as her own preserve. The province of Asia was wealthy and therefore enormously profitable, and could not be given up lightly. There were no Roman armies to stop Mithridates on the spot, so the search began for a suitable general to send against him.

This was where Sulla and Marius clashed, because both of them wanted the command. In the end Sulla obtained it, and left Rome to the mercy of his opponents. One of the consuls for 87 was Lucius Cornelius Cinna, who brought Marius back to Rome. Between them they proscribed and caused the massacre of leading senators who were considered dangerous. The casualties included the senior members of Antony's family on both his mother's and his father's side. The elder Marcus Antonius has already been mentioned. Another victim was Lucius Julius Caesar (distantly related to Gaius Julius Caesar). This man was the father of Julia, Antony's mother. Thus by the time that Antony was born, both his maternal and paternal grandfathers were dead, a factor which would have a considerable part to play in Antony's make-up. Family ideology would provide him with a knowledge of the dangers of associating with the wrong factions, and the advantages of seeking inclusion in the right ones. It was rapidly becoming clear that neutrality was not an option for men who wanted to rise via a senatorial career.

When Sulla returned to Rome in 83, another civil war broke out between his partisans and those of Marius. In this context a young general rose to fame by raising a private army from among his tenants on his estates in Picenum, and leading it in support of Sulla. This was Gnaeus Pompey, soon to add the epithet Magnus, 'the Great', to his name. Modesty never helped anyone in the Roman world, so Pompey never cultivated it. By a combination of self-advertisement and military successes Pompey became one of the most powerful men that Rome had ever seen. He took his first steps to fame in the shadow of Sulla, who was made Dictator and set about overhauling the state, placing the Senate firmly in control and wresting power from the people. When his work was done Sulla laid down his office and retired, an action which Julius Caesar could not comprehend, and labelled ill-advised and foolish. The way was now cleared for the rise of Pompey, who was removed from the immediate political scene for the time being to go and fight the rebel

Quintus Sertorius, who had set himself up as a virtual autocrat in Spain. Pompey was thus occupied from 77 to 73.

While the Spanish war was going on, Marcus Antonius, the father of three boys — Mark Antony and his younger brothers Gaius and Lucius — was praetor in 74. At the end of his term he was given a command against the pirates in Crete, but he enjoyed little success. He earned the nickname Creticus, which would normally signify a victorious campaign, but in his case denoted defeat. He was killed while still in office in 71. Antony, now aged about 11, was fatherless, and moreover had to live down the fact that his father had been defeated in battle, left the family in debt, and had never been particularly noteworthy under any heading. Stories are told of Antony's father, impulsive, generous, disorganised, and ultimately a failure, and the stories were readily accepted because they demonstrate so aptly the old adage 'like father, like son'. One of the most famous tales demonstrates his fecklessness and also his generosity. A friend called on him to ask for a loan, but Antonius had no money to spare. Resourceful as well as irresponsible, he sent a slave to fetch a silver dish, which he presented to his friend, telling him to sell it and keep the money. All went well until some time later, when Julia missed the dish and started to question the slaves, accusing them of theft, at which point Antonius confessed his guilt. Julia's reaction is not recorded, but the unwritten sub-text is that she was accustomed to this behaviour and perhaps condoned it, making the best of the situation in which she found herself.

As a widow with three young sons, Julia did not remain unmarried for long. Her next husband was Publius Cornelius Lentulus Sura, a senator of some standing, who was consul in 71. It was therefore a good match. Antony and his brothers were brought up in Lentulus' house, and they seem to have been fond of their stepfather. It could have been the beginning of a significant career for Antony, if only Lentulus had been in the right faction. In 70, he was ejected from the Senate by the censors, in a biased but perfectly legal purge. The consuls for that year were Pompey and Marcus Licinius Crassus whose recent exploits gave them the dubious distinction of saving the state from the slave army led by Spartacus. Crassus had done most of the work, and Pompey had mopped up the remnants as they fled northwards into the path of his army returning from Spain. Although a victory, it was not considered glorious because slaves were not supposed to be worthy enemies of Rome. Pompey's reputation as a general was secure, but Crassus had not enjoyed the same experience, and therefore continually sought a more dignified command that would bestow upon him the military distinction that he craved. His candidacy for the consulship was perfectly legitimate, but the Senate distrusted him. Pompey, as always, was in an anomalous position. Up to now his career had been quite abnormal. He had not held any of the requisite preliminary offices, having bypassed the quaestorship and praetorship and gone on to become a self-appointed general instead. Consequently he had no administrative experience, and he had to persuade his literary friend Varro to write a little handbook for him on senatorial procedure. Moreover he was under age, and not only that, he was quite blatantly intent on destroying Sulla's work in strengthening the Senate. As part of this policy he needed to disempower Sulla's supporters and anyone who had not demonstrated loyalty to his own party. It was at Pompey's insistence that censors were appointed to revise the list of senators. At least his malice was confined to the ruination of men's careers, rather than the eradication of potential opposition by proscriptions. Lentulus Sura and Antony's uncle Gaius Antonius Hybrida were forced out of the Senate, and had to begin their careers all over again.

As a young man, Antony's circumstances were far from ideal, conveying no hope of a brilliant future. His real father had left considerable debts, so Antony started life as a bankrupt. Now the brief promise of salvation was gone, since his stepfather Lentulus was pushed far back along the path to a lucrative career. It was too late now to begin to make overtures to the one man in Rome who counted for anything, and perhaps by inclination Lentulus did not wish to associate with Pompey. By 63 he had worked his way upwards and had become urban praetor, which was a lowly enough post for a man who had been consul eight years earlier. While he was growing up, Antony would have become increasingly aware of factional strife in Rome, and by observation he would note how it was possible to rise to power via command of armed forces. A successful general would always be popular whenever there were enemies to fight, so Pompey went from strength to strength. First he had himself appointed to command against the pirates in the Mediterranean, for which he needed special dispensation to grant him the power and authorisation to give orders to the provincial governors of territories all round the periphery of the sea, which was in effect most of the whole Roman world. Such an extended command made perfect sense, since the piecemeal attempts to eradicate the pirates had so far proved ineffective, or only temporarily successful. There was a definite need for an extensive unified command, but it set a dangerous precedent. Pompey was as good as his word. He divided the Mediterranean into sectors, placed squadrons in each of them, and made rapid sweeps of them all. In less than two months he had rounded up all the pirates and made the Roman world safe, securing the food supply in the process. His next project was even more ambitious. He angled to deprive Lucullus of the eastern command against Mithridates, where the campaign was not going well. Between 66 and 63, Pompey brought forcible peace to the eastern provinces and made arrangements for the future administration of the whole area.

Meanwhile events at Rome moved on apace. There were many discontented men in the city. One of them was Crassus, the consular colleague of Pompey, who envisaged his own reputation constantly whittled away by

Pompey's resounding and continuing successes, and schemed to add military glory to his vast fortune, in order to provide a counterweight to the overbearing influence of the Pompeians in Rome. Another restless soul was the new man called Marcus Tullius Cicero, regarded with disdain by the establishment, who was gaining fame via his work in the law courts and was clearly aiming for the consulship. The most dangerous of all was a rising politician, a relative of Gaius Marius,who was seeking power in whatever way he could get it, and was drawn to Crassus as his financial backer. This was Gaius Julius Caesar, not yet a name to reckon with in Roman politics. Besides these ambitious men there were many dispossessed and impoverished citizens in Rome, Marians who had suffered at the hands of Sulla, and those like Antony's stepfather and uncle who had fallen victim to Pompey's purge of the Senate. The situation was ripe for rebellion for any number of personal or political reasons. All that was required was a suitably qualified and disgruntled leader to take up an inflammatory cause, and such a man emerged in the form of Lucius Sergius Catilina, who was thwarted of the consulship in 65. He presented himself as a candidate for the elections in 64 for the consulship of 63. The other candidates were Antony's uncle Gaius Antonius Hybrida and Cicero. The Senate was presented with a problem. The senators did not really want any of these candidates. They would tolerate Hybrida, but they did not want Cicero. Their dilemma was that they wanted Catilina even less, so Hybrida was duly elected along with Cicero, who therefore achieved his life's ambition by default as the best of a bad lot.

Until now Catilina had enjoyed the financial support of Crassus, but Crassus did not back losers for long, so his support was withdrawn. Desperate now, Catilina started to raise troops. Having failed to attain power by legitimate political means he resorted to armed force. This is where Antony's stepfather enters the scene. Lentulus tried to subvert a party of Allobroges from Gaul, who had come to Rome to seek redress for wrongs from the Senate. When they were unsuccessful, Lentulus judged that they might be converted to the cause, and if so, then they could perhaps provide some of their famed mounted warriors to add to Catilina's growing army. He miscalculated. After some soul-searching the Allobroges informed on him, but meanwhile played the parts of double agents, leading the conspirators on until the case was quite clear. Catilina escaped to fight again, but the ringleaders were arrested and brought before the Senate. Julius Caesar, who was now Pontifex Maximus or High Priest, spoke in favour of a mild penalty, namely imprisonment under close supervision in the Italian towns. No-one heeded him because hysteria had taken too strong a hold. The moment was Cicero's finest hour. He had discovered a conspiracy, patiently watched it grow until it reached the point of no return, then he had arrested the culprits, and he was not to be cheated of their deaths. He carried the day, and the conspirators were executed, Lentulus among them. Cicero ought to have gone through laborious legal procedure and arranged for prosecution and defence, but he was in too much of a hurry, perhaps because as a lawyer he knew that there were many problems to be encountered between prosecution and conviction. Condemnation was not a foregone conclusion, especially if a brilliant speaker could be found to plead the cause of the conspirators. If Cicero risked going through the proper procedure, the end result might be very far from the punishment he so desired.

After the executions, Antony always declared that Lentulus' body was not released to the family for proper burial except after an interview with Cicero's wife. Ancient authors did not believe the story, since as far as they were concerned all the criminals were allowed decent funerals. This may be quite true, but misses the point. Antony believed that Cicero would go so far as to deny his stepfather a Roman funeral. The truth is of no importance. Antony was about 19 years old, grieving for his stepfather and distressed on account of the suffering of his mother. He had no money, no career prospects, and had perhaps been a party to the despair that drove Lentulus to try to alter the way the state was functioning. All that Antony would be able to see was a man who had enjoyed an honourable career suddenly blocked from promotion, and then cut down when he tried to protest. Logic would not enter into his calculations; the man who had caused the death of his stepfather without a fair trial was Marcus Tullius Cicero, a new man from outside Rome, who was no better than the Antonii or the family of Lentulus. It was unlikely that Antony would ever forgive him.

Two important characters had now entered Antony's life, and from now on would have considerable influence on his future. Cicero was already an enemy. But the incident had also produced a potential ally. Gaius Julius Caesar had risked his reputation and perhaps even his life by speaking in favour of a lighter penalty for the conspirators. He could have jeopardised his own career, or found himself accused of complicity in the plot, but nonetheless he spoke out in public, in effect pleading for the lives of condemned men. It is not recorded that Antony and Caesar met at this time, but Antony would have taken note of the name.

Possibly at this time, while Catilina was still at large, Antony married for the first time, though some authors put the marriage much later in 53 or 52. His bride was his cousin Antonia, daughter of the consul Gaius Antonius Hybrida. This individual had a shady reputation. He was also a born survivor. Ejected from the Senate in 70, he began his career again, becoming praetor in 66, reaching the consulship with Cicero as colleague in 63, but both of them were elected largely as a stopgap chosen by the Senate to prevent Catilina from attaining the office. When the news of the conspiracy broke out, he tried to remain on the fence, but was finally forced into activity to avoid charges of sympathisisng with the conspirators. In 62 he took the field at the head of an army against Catilina, but the battle was won by his legate Marcus Petreius, because Hybrida was laid low by an attack of gout. Despite his action, suspicion still attached to Hybrida, and so marriage into this family was not necessarily a profitable alliance for Antony. His new wife seems to have made little impression on him, and marriage certainly did not convert him into a sedate family man. His youth was joyously frittered away in drinking, gambling and womanising, in the company of his great friend Gaius Scribonius Curio, who was just as badly behaved, but wealthier and better connected, and therefore much more likely to emerge unscathed. Some ancient authors blame Curio for leading Antony astray, but it is highly unlikely that Antony needed any encouragement in this sphere. It is characteristic of him that he tried to match expense for expense and escapade for escapade, with no thought for the consequences. Proudly he refused to sit in the seats at the theatre reserved for bankrupts, while at the same time incurring more and more debts. Anyone who has ever been in a similar position will know that there comes a point where more debts cease to mean anything. The remoteness of being able to repay any of the money simply invites further recklessness. Curio offered to stand surety for Antony's debts, a gesture not to be underestimated, and testimony to Antony's capacity to inspire friendship. The plan did not work, because Curio's father found out, and banished Antony from the house and his son's presence. The scenario has a modern flavour, familiar to all societies in all ages.

Antony never renounced Curio's friendship altogether, remaining on good terms with him until the latter's death. Cicero in the *Philippics* accuses Antony of homosexual relations with Curio, going on to suggest that to many other young men he actually sold his favours, but this was a standard derogatory charge that lost much of its impact through indiscriminate overuse. Caesar was accused of the same thing, and so was Octavian — by Antony himself, when the two were battling for supremacy after Caesar's death. Deprived of Curio's company in his youth, Antony turned to another reprobate called Publius Claudius Pulcher, who changed his name in 59 to the plebeian form of Clodius, by which name he is known to posterity. His behaviour was always scandalous. He was said to have penetrated the festival celebrated in honour of the Bona Dea, observed exclusively by women. In order to carry out his design, whatever it was, he dressed as a woman, but was discovered by Caesar's mother Aurelia, in whose house the ceremony was held. It was said that he was trying to conduct an affair with Caesar's wife Pompeia, so Caesar divorced her, saying that 'Caesar's wife should be above suspicion'. A great deal of suspicion attaches to the incident; Caesar would not assist Cicero in the prosecution of Clodius, for reasons best known to himself. The only result was that Clodius became a bitter enemy of Cicero.

Antony's activities are not documented during these years. He would certainly have met Clodius' wife Fulvia, and may even have begun an affair with her, mainly because he could not see a woman without thinking of the bedroom first and intellectual pursuits second. Fulvia may have attracted him for all the elevated reasons as well as sex, since he eventually married her, and seems to have been fond of her to the point of indulgence. Apart from these few conjectures virtually nothing is known of Antony's life at this period. He would be a witness to the return of Pompey in 63, and would learn from the experience. Pompey did not march on Rome at the head of his troops but disbanded them quietly and then entered Rome, confident that the sheer magnitude of his achievements and his undoubted supremacy would facilitate all his eastern administrative arrangements and the provision of land allotments for his veterans. He was to be sadly disillusioned. He had enriched the Roman Treasury by enormous amounts, but got no credit for it, and the Senate would not ratify his acts without first debating endlessly each minor point. More and more frustrated and beginning to lose face, Pompey was drawn towards Crassus and Caesar, all of whom needed each other in some way to advance their own careers. Crassus and Pompey were old rivals but sank their differences. Caesar had meanwhile launched himself on his political career. He had been praetor in 62 and governor of Further Spain from 61 to 60, and in that short time he had managed to raise the cash to pay off most of his considerable debts. On his return he demanded a triumph for his military exploits in peace-making in the province, and also the right to stand for the consulship of 59. As a returning general at the head of an army he was not allowed to enter the city, so he kicked his heels while the Senate considered and then refused his request for a triumph. Quite unruffled, he readily abandoned the idea of holding a triumph, and threw himself instead into the more important matter of the consulship, backed by Pompey and Crassus. He was duly elected with Bibulus as colleague, but he was soon acting almost independently, ignoring Bibulus and most of the Senate. Roman wits referred to the consulship of Julius and Caesar, instead of Caesar and Bibulus.

Not all Caesar's actions were selfish, even though he acted in a blatantly dictatorial manner. His capacity for recognising the need for administrative reforms and then for pushing them through revealed itself very early. Pompey's eastern arrangements were ratified en bloc, at last. A dynastic marriage was arranged to bind Pompey and Caesar closer together. Pompey had divorced his wife Mucia as soon as he returned to Rome, and was now the most eligible bachelor in the world, so Caesar offered him the hand of his only child, Julia. The match was a successful one; Pompey was known to dote on his new wife. Caesar himself arranged his own appointment to the province of Cisalpine Gaul and Illyricum, which would once again give him command of troops. The command was extended when the governor of Transalpine

1.   *Head of Gaius Julius Caesar, Antony's mentor, who appointed him to his first independent commands in Gaul. There was a distant family relationship between them through Antony's mother Julia, the daughter of Lucius Julius Caesar.*

Courtesy Vatican Museums, Vatican City

Gaul died in office, and at Pompey's suggestion the extra province was granted to Caesar with one more legion. The conquest of Gaul laid a firm foundaton for Caesar's supremacy.

The unofficial alliance between Crassus, Pompey and Caesar had proved itself stronger than the Senate. It remained to reduce the power of their individual and mutual rivals. To this end Cato, who had delighted in dissecting each and every one of Pompey's eastern administrative arrangements, and Cicero were removed from Rome. Cato went on a legitimate errand to take over Cyprus. Cicero was banished due to the machinations of the newly appointed tribune of the plebs, Clodius. Caesar had presided over the necessary adoption of Clodius into a plebeian family, since as a patrician he was not eligible for the tribunate. It was an absolutely shameless piece of unscrupulous manipulation of the regulations, for purely personal and selfish reasons. Once in office, Clodius passed a law that was aimed directly at Cicero. Anyone who had put to death Roman citizens without due process of law was to be outlawed. Cicero now most likely bitterly resented his haste in executing the conspirators. The political climate in Rome was such that he suddenly found himself out on a limb with no friends; he tried to visit Pompey who saw him approaching, and fled by the back door as Cicero was shown in at the front. Before he could be prosecuted, Cicero went into exile at Thessalonika. His banishment was formally ratifed after his departure, and his houses were destroyed. He was convinced that Antony had been one of the prime movers behind his banishment. This may have been true, but it is far from certain that Antony had any influence whatsoever at this stage and, in any case, Cicero had made himself an enemy of too many people to require Antony's assistance in his loss of favour. Whether or not he was party to Cicero's fate, it is not likely that Antony would have shed any tears of sympathy. He probably went out to get a girl and hopelessly drunk, in that order.

Caesar waited in Rome until Cicero had left Italy and then departed for Gaul. In that same year, 58, Antony went to Greece, to study at Athens and Rhodes. It was said that he had tired of Clodius' excesses. He may have had enough presence of mind to see disaster looming. Pompey was in charge in Rome, and that had not helped Lentulus Sura or Antony's uncle the last time that Pompey enjoyed unrivalled power. It seems that there had been a rift of some sort between Clodius and Antony; when they met in Rome years later, Antony threatened his erstwhile friend with violence. At any rate it is fortunate that Antony had quite decidedly detached himself from the entourage of Clodius well before the latter was attacked and killed by his rival Milo in 52. Fulvia did not remain a widow for very long. She married Antony's friend Curio.

At Athens, Antony's course of study, according to Plutarch, consisted of military excercises and the practice of the florid Asiatic style of oratory which was so suited to Antony's character, being full of swagger and melodrama. His grandfather had been a distinguished orator, a fact which Antony would have absorbed as part of his family history. His academic progress is unknown, but at the same time there are no stories that he deflowered too many Athenian virgins or wrecked too many Athenian taverns. It is at least possible that he suffered somewhat from depression, having no particular aims in life, and no money to render the aimlessness palatable. His ambitions were tested when Aulus Gabinius arrived in Greece on his way to take up his post as governor of Syria. He invited Antony to accompany him, but could not tempt him with the offer of an administrative post. When he talked real sense and offered Antony the command of the cavalry, the young man came into his own. Whatever he had decided on as his future, it was crystallised now, when he left Greece with Gabinius, to find romance and adventure as a cavalry commander.

They travelled together to Antioch, where they were greeted with the news that there was a civil war in Judaea. The situation there was volatile, and called for Roman intervention, to protect the interests of Rome as much as the citizens of Judaea. It was within the brief of the governor of Syria to interfere in Judaean affairs and to re-establish order. The problem dated back to Pompey's conquest. The Roman favourite was Hyrcanus, who was both High Priest and ruler, but he was opposed by Alexander, the son of Aristobalus, who was languishing at Pompey' pleasure in prison in Rome. Once in Judaea, Antony was sent ahead with the cavalry and some light armed infantry to find Alexander's rebel army, and then to wait for the arrival of the Roman troops. There were two battles, one near Jerusalem and one on the road to Jericho, in which Antony distiguished himself. It must be remembered that he had had no formal military training to speak of except the rudimentary excercises that Roman boys went through, and his studies at Athens. At some point he had absorbed how to ride a horse, how to command men who may well have been more practised than he was himself, and what to do in emergencies.

Peace was restored for a short time, only to be disturbed all over again when Aristobalus escaped from Rome and tried to re-establish himself in Judaea. This time Gabinius stayed at Antioch and sent three commanders, one of whom was Antony, to deal with the situation. When Aristobalus was forced to fall back on the ruins of Machaerus, Antony led the assault on the town. He had thus revealed qualities of bravery and leadership, had gained the respect of the soldiers, and also experience of eastern affairs. He was to widen this experience in the next few months, entering Egypt and a world that was to have a great bearing on his future. As yet Rome had no direct means of controlling Egypt, but indirectly she already controlled much of what went on in the kingdom, because Roman influence had become the dominant factor in

Egyptian politics. While Caesar was consul in 59, he and Pompey had established Ptolemy Auletes ('the flute player') on the Egyptian throne, at a price. In order to pay this price, Ptolemy increased existing taxes and raised new ones, which made him so unpopular that he was forced to flee to Rome to seek help. Pompey was sympathetic, but the Senate was not, and at this stage Pompey was not willing to compromise himself. Hence Ptolemy turned up at Gabinius' headquarters in Antioch, seeking military assistance, which he promised to pay for. Tacitly, Pompey condoned the idea, and Gabinius was Pompey's man. Technically, Gabinius had no authority to intervene; it was illegal for him to enter Egypt at all, much less invade with an army, but tempted by the fabulous wealth of the country, and egged on by Antony who detected a whiff of romance and adventure, in 55 Gabinus set about putting Ptolemy back on his throne.

It is not an easy task to invade Egypt by land, since it is protected on both sides by deserts, and the Nile Delta is an obstacle in itself, especially when patrolled by watchful ships. Antony crossed the desert with few casualties, and captured Pelusium, the gateway to Alexandria. He was instrumental in preventing a vengeful massacre of the inhabitants by Ptolemy, and thereby earned himself a reputation for courage and fair play. From Pelusium the Roman army fought and skirmished its way to Alexandria, where Antony stayed for a while, impressing the inhabitants and the Roman soldiers with his exploits. He was 28 years old, with a body like an athlete, which he liked to show off by wearing very short tunics; he was popular with his men, an acknowledged womaniser, generous to a fault, and he could drink anybody under the table. It is possible that he may have met the princess Cleopatra while he was in Alexandria. She was about 13 years old. If they did meet, it is unlikely that they would have made much impression on each other. By origin, upbringing, education, and ambitions, they were poles apart. It was much later, when mutual needs drew them together, that the eternal combination began.

2 Caesar

Antony's stay in Egypt was brief, and confined to restoring Ptolemy Auletes on his throne. A second revolt against Hyrcanus broke out in spring 55, so Gabinius marched his troops once again to Judaea, Antony and the cavalry included. When the revolt was put down, Gabinius returned to Syria. Antony remained there for another year, without recorded incident. There had been significant developments in Rome. Cicero had returned from exile, recalled by the efforts of Pompey. In 56, Caesar had taken time off from the conquest of Gaul, and travelled to Cisalpine Gaul to meet Crassus. They probably worked out a few mutually beneficial schemes before they went together to Luca to meet Pompey. They all brought their followers with them, who crowded the little town while their masters, holding their meetings in secret, arranged the fate of the world. The three men between them possessed enough corporate influence to ensure that whatever they desired would happen, even to the extent of engineering the elections of magistrates. It was agreed that Crassus and Pompey should become consuls for 55, and that Caesar should be confirmed as governor of Gaul for another five years. He had no intention of leaving the conquest half finished, because that would give someone else the chance to mop up what he had begun, and then take all the credit for it. Caesar possessed a fully developed sense of his own importance, and it was not part of his plan even to share the credit, much less allow someone to take it.

Crassus was already making plans for his proconsulship. Originally he was to govern Spain and Pompey was to go to Syria, but these arrangements were reversed. Crassus saw his chance to make his mark. As governor of Syria, he intended to conquer Parthia, the one power that could rival or even outshine Rome in the extent of her Empire and in her sophisticated organisation. He began to recruit an army while he was still consul, and took over Gabinius' troops when he arrived in Syria, not without a struggle, because at first Gabinius refused to hand over his command. Antony left Syria in the same year that Crassus arrived, but the chronology is not clear. It is not established whether Antony was offered any post under Crassus, or whether he simply did not want to serve under him. Evidently he had decided that his future lay

2. *Head of Mark Antony from Rome. Since Antony's memory was damned after his death and his portraits and statues were destroyed, the identification of what remains is hazardous. Though this head has been damaged, it still shows some of the characteristics of Antony's coin portraits, with its determined stare, thickset neck and square-jawed, fleshy face.*

Courtesy Capitoline Museum, Rome

in independent action. He did not find a post with Crassus, nor did he return to Rome in the entourage of Gabinius, who was prosecuted as soon as he reached Rome for leading his army out of Syria without authorisation from the Senate. On that charge Gabinius was acquitted, but was then promptly charged again on the grounds that he had accepted bribes from Ptolemy. Cicero undertook the defence, against his will and not very well. Gabinius went into exile. Perhaps with a sense of self-preservation, Antony did not appear in Rome. It is said that he dared not face his creditors, which is quite likely, but it is also likely that in addition he knew that the Egyptian venture would draw criticism if not prosecution, and since he had been the very person who had spoken for the scheme, advising Gabinius to undertake it, perhaps he deemed it wise to find employment elsewhere.

He went from Syria to Gaul, via the overland route through Asia Minor and Greece. Presumably he did not simply set off on this journey vaguely hoping that Caesar would welcome him. Before he left Syria, or while he was travelling, he will have contacted Caesar himself, or possibly one of the Caesarian generals in Gaul who could lay his case before Caesar. Perhaps he sent the equivalent of a C.V. along with his letter, pointing out that he was now much more experienced than the rowdy youth that Caesar would remember from his days in Rome. He had gained a classical education in Athens and Rhodes, he had studied oratory and with it the means of verbal persuasion that would be necessary in his political career. More important, he had gained valuable knowledge of armies and how they functioned, and had acquitted himself well in battle. The details of Antony's journey to Gaul and Caesar's opinion of him before and after he arrived there have not been recorded. Somehow and at some date, he reached Caesar and became part of his army. What he did for the next couple of years is not known, but he soon rose to a position of importance as one of Caesar's generals, sometimes entrusted with semi-independent commands which called for initiative and courage. How he arrived at this position of trusted officer is not documented. He served an unrecorded two-year apprenticeship under the eye of Caesar, and presumably impressed the general sufficiently to gain promotion; at any rate, by the time he entered history, via Caesar's commentaries on the Gallic war, Antony was a fully-fledged lieutenant in command of troops. The first mention of Antony by name in these commentaries is at the siege of Alesia, when Antony and Trebonius, called *legati* or legates, shrewdly anticipated trouble and kept troops at the ready, with which they were able to fight off a night attack on the siege works.

The years which Antony spent in Gaul with Caesar were eventful ones for Rome. The marriage alliance between Caesar and Pompey was severed when Julia died in childbirth in 54. The child died too, so there was no family connection to be preserved that may have bound the two men together.

Though Julia's death did not create an immediate rift between Pompey and Caesar, it removed a potential link and a possible soothing influence which her presence might have exerted upon her father and husband when it came to open war. The situation did not deteriorate overnight, but an almost inexorable, if gradual, rivalry was bound to separate Rome's greatest general from the brilliant, determined, ruthless, self-advertising, conqueror of Gaul. A year after the death of Julia, Marcus Licinius Crassus, the other rather less stable link between Pompey and Caesar, was removed from the scene, disastrously defeated and horrifically killed in Parthia. His dream of conquering the Parthian Empire was shattered; Crassus lost his army and died swallowing molten gold, forced down his throat by the Parthians in reference to his love of wealth.

The Parthians were Rome's most organised enemy, and also the most glamorous, redolent of Alexander the Great and his eastern conquests. Antony was young, adventurous, and romantic; and he knew something of the east already. All the substance that he needed for the development of a romantic dream of his own was in place. The defeat and death of Crassus begged for revenge, and the stain on Rome's prowess and military reputation could only be removed by a resounding victory. Perhaps it was now, when the news reached him of the disaster, that Antony began to formulate plans of his own for a Parthian expedition to end all Parthian expeditions. He may have discussed the problem with Caesar, playing the Roman equivalent of war-gaming in conversations at dinner. The topic was probably never allowed to go out of fashion; when he was murdered in March 44, Caesar was about to set out on a campaign on the Danube which he intended to follow up with another against Parthia. He had raised the troops and the cash, and a few months earlier he had sent his great-nephew Gaius Octavius to Macedonia where five legions were stationed in readiness. It is likely that Caesar planned to take Antony with him to Parthia, and may have talked to him about the country and the enemy army. If he knew at least something of Caesar's plans, Antony probably thought of himself as the heir to these projected conquests; at any rate it is highly unlikely that he ever forgot Crassus' Parthian disaster.

As long as Caesar devoted himself single-mindedly to the conquest of Gaul, the possibility of conflict between him and Pompey was postponed. Everything depended on what happened when Caesar's term as governor expired; he waited upon events and did not yet show his hand. In the meantime he fostered Antony's career, allowing him to go to Rome in 53 to stand as a candidate for the quaestorship for 52. Antony was duly elected, at least partly on his own merits, but doubtless mostly because of Caesar's overt support. He went to see Cicero, who refers to the visit in the *Philippics*, revealing that Caesar had written to him to ask him to receive Antony and support him for the quaestorship. Thus Antony was now properly launched upon his political career, and indelibly dyed as one of Caesar's protégés. During the winter of 52/1 he was put in charge of the winter quarters near Bibracte (modern Autun), while Caesar went off on a rapid campaign in December against the Bituriges, whose lands were fertile and well-populated, and therefore provided a lucrative source of wealth and supplies. Antony probably saw no action until Caesar called him to his side to take command of the XII legion in a campaign against the Eburones, who dwelt between the river Meuse and the Rhine. Antony remained in northern Gaul, in command of 15 cohorts, or the equivalent of one and a half legions. It was in this part of Gaul, just south of the Rhine, that the last spark of Gallic resistance to Caesar and Roman domination finally died out. For some time Commius, the leader of the Atrebates, had resisted the Roman advance, taking advantage of his position to liaise with the Germanic peoples across the Rhine, whose aid he sought more than once in his struggle. When threatened with defeat or capture he simply fled across the Rhine to his allies, remaining just beyond the reach of the Roman legions. He was a constant thorn in Caesar's side, clever, resourceful and justifiably bitter. He had made the mistake in the previous year of agreeing to talk to the Roman envoy Gaius Volusenus, not knowing that Caesar's friend and trusted lieutenant, Titus Labienus, had arranged an ambush. Fortunately for Commius and unfortunately for Caesar, the centurion appointed to despatch the leader of the Atrebates bungled the job, so Commius got away with a head wound and a lifelong grudge.

As commander of the northern region, Antony soon came into conflict with Commius, who used his swift horsemen in a perpetual guerilla war, threatening communications and supply lines. Gaius Volusenus was now Antony's cavalry commander, and was given the task of frustrating Commius' raids. The two met in a skirmish, in which Commius personally led the charge against the Roman horsemen, succeeding in wounding Volusenus in the thigh. Despite this success, he eventually came to terms with Antony, sending hostages to him as guarantee for his peaceful behaviour. Unfortunately it is not known what part Antony played in bringing about this capitulation. He perhaps simply took advantage of Commius' increasingly difficult circumstances, waiting patiently until it became obvious that the raiders could not remain welded together for long, and their guerilla war could not be sustained. On more than one occasion Antony made correct decisons based on an accurate judgement of the enemy situation, either because he operated an efficient intelligence service, or on account of his own powers of deduction, or both. Commius eventually migrated to Britain, and the peoples of Gaul finally accepted Roman rule. Antony's contribution in ending the war may not have been of resounding military or historical importance, but it reveals that he could act on his own initiative and was trusted to do so. He had progressed far beyond the youthful cavalry commander in Syria.

Caesar's support and encouragement were no doubt the prime considerations behind Antony's election as augur for 50. This was a religious office which he retained all his life. He may have sought the appointment in 53, because a vacancy had occurred after the death of Crassus' son in Parthia. If he stood for the office at that time he clearly did not obtain it. In 50 there was another vacancy when the orator Quintus Hortensius died, and on this occasion Antony was successfully elected. Caesar canvassed for his election vigorously, and as usual, Caesar's support won the day. Antony's main rival was Domitius, whose candidacy was favoured by Cato and the senatorial party, anti-Caesarians to the last man, so Antony's success was all the more remarkable, but at this period Caesar experienced no difficulty in putting candidates of his own into political or religious offices. The duties of the augurs were to observe and interpret the heavenly signs from the gods, which could be revealed to them in the skies or in the flights of birds. Taking the auspices, or divination of the will of the gods, was an important feature of Roman life, rooted in the distant past; the word auspices derives from *auspicium* or *avispicium*, denoting the observation of birds (*avis* means bird and *specio* means I look, or I see). No magistrate would embark on serious business without taking the auspices first, so the augurs who were entrusted with interpretation of the signs could exert significant power over public life, because if they considered that the omens were unfavourable they could suspend all public business, or even retrospectively invalidate actions or decisions that had already been taken. With Antony as augur, there would have been several advantages of which Caesar could avail himself if ever need arose, even if only to extricate himself from temporary difficulties. For Antony, the appointment was not just an empty honour; it was a useful political tool. Whether he had any formal training in how to observe and interpret the movements of birds is largely irrelevant. It is perhaps unfair to question his integrity too closely, but it is almost certain that without the slightest hesitation, he would interpret the signs in accordance with Caesar's wishes.

Antony's appointment as augur was aided and abetted by his old friend Curio, who was tribune in the year of the elections. He too was Caesar's man, so the two friends worked towards the same end, protecting Caesar's interests. When Curio's tribuneship came to an end, it was important to replace him for the new term with a compliant Caesarian, so Antony in his turn became tribune, taking up office in December 50, for the following year. It was a crucial one for Caesar. The problems over his tenure of Gaul had already begun in 51 when the anti-Caesarian consul Marcellus suggested that Caesar should be recalled in that year. Pompey tried to put an end to vacillation and uncertainty, and opted for a definite terminal date of 1 March 50, on the sensible grounds that the command of Gaul had been granted to Caesar for a second term of five years in 55. This postponed the thorny decision for a while, and clung firmly to the letter of the law, if such a description can be applied to the more or less private agreement that had engineered the extension of Caesar's governorship. Whenever the matter was raised thereafter, Curio as tribune vetoed the proceedings if there was the slightest hint of a threat to Caesar, but such a state of affairs could not continue indefinitely. Caesar's enemies manoeuvred to find a new loophole as fast as his friends manoeuvred to close the last one. It was clear that there would be a clash of some kind between Pompey and Caesar, who could not work together any longer as equals. The state was not big enough to accommodate both of them. A dangerous precedent had been set of allowing Pompey to be consul while at the same time commanding troops; such an anomaly had not been condoned in the past, and it now gave Caesar the excuse to claim that if he came to Rome to stand for the consulship, disbanding his army as he was legally obliged to do, then he was potentially at risk from Pompey's troops, and unfairly bereft of any protection of his own.

Caesar retained his post as proconsul of Gaul throughout the political ups and downs in Rome. The terminal date suggested by Pompey of 1 March 50 came and went without the outbreak of serious hostilities. On 1 December 50, Caesar offered a compromise solution, through the agency of Curio: he would disband his army before he entered Rome to stand for the consulship, if Pompey would also disband his troops as a reciprocal gesture. Many senators approved of this plan but the consuls sabotaged it. Marcellus over-reacted and asked Pompey to assume command of all the troops in Italy. There followed a proposal in January 49 that Caesar should be forced to disband his army by a certain date or be declared an enemy of the state. The tribunes Mark Antony and Quintus Cassius vetoed the proposal, but feelings were running very high, and the Senate was not willing to compromise. Antony and Cassius were thrown out of the Senate House, and threatened with death if they tried to re-enter. They left Rome in a hurry, disguised as slaves, and made their way to Caesar.

When they arrived at Caesar's camp, dishevelled and tired, Caesar quickly grasped the opportunity to show them to the troops in their sorry state, to demonstrate just how shabbily they had been treated. He had all the evidence that he needed to work up the soldiers with the news that Antony and Cassius, trying to protect the interests of Caesar and therefore of the army, had been forcibly ejected from the Senate and hounded out of Rome in fear for their lives. Not only that, but Caesar was now declared a public enemy and by extension of that idea the soldiers too were enemies. This was their reward for fighting hard for Rome for the past eight or nine years — to be declared enemies and therefore outlaws. Having dealt with the soldiers, Caesar attended to his civilian and political image. He acted as he did, he said, to protect the sacrosanctity of the tribunes. Antony and Cassius were the sacrosanct representatives of the people, yet they had been treated abysmally. On this lofty political pretext, Caesar took his army across the river Rubicon, which separated his province from Italy. To do so was an unequivocal declaration of war.

Antony was amost immediately sent off on an independent mission, to secure Arezzo with five cohorts under his command, while Caesar raised troops elsewhere. When the town was won, and Caesar had his troops, the two reunited 93 miles (150km) from Rome at Corfinium. Already one of Caesar's trusted lieutenants, Antony may have been drawn closer to Caesar after the departure of Titus Labienus. Until now Labienus had always been associated with Caesar, but he came from the same part of the world as Pompey, and now his allegiance changed. He joined the Pompeians and from then onwards he was the most implacable of Caesar's enemies. He may have been jealous of Antony, whose promotion came without long and hard service in the army. No-one knows why Labienus left Caesar when the civil war began. Pompey meanwhile had been caught off guard by Caesar's rapid advance from the north. He had done nothing to raise an effective army, having proclaimed proudly but misguidedly that he only had to stamp his foot and troops would spring up in Italy. Stamp as he would, few troops sprang up. Having no army of sufficient calibre to match Caesar's, Pompey abandoned Rome and withdrew to the south. He needed to delay the start of the war, and take time to train his army. Eventually he set sail from Brundisium and transferred the whole of his army to Greece. Many senators, forced to make a choice, followed him. Caesar was now supreme in Italy, but he was flanked on east and west by armed enemies. Pompey was governor of Spain in absentia, so the troops there were loyal to him, and decided to hold the province for him. Caesar acted decisively. He decided to deal with Spain first, summing up the situation with one of his usual succinct phrases: 'I go to fight an army with no commander, then I will deal with the commander with no army.'

Antony was left in command of Italy as *magister equitum*, or master of horse. Though the title might suggest that he had merely re-assumed his role as a cavalry commander, his task was much more wide-ranging and more important than that. He was in charge of all troops in Italy and by dint of his overall military command he was in control of the government of Italy, with the exception of the city of Rome, where Marcus Aemilius Lepidus as urban praetor was responsible for day to day administration. Antony had little experience in this sphere; he was still legally and officially tribune until December 49, but not having held any of the higher offices his knowledge of administration was not as great as his military capabilities. Caesar had given him the task most suited to him. He was quite capable of keeping order, both among the civilian communities and in the army. Energetic and committed, Antony fulfilled his duties with determination and vigour, but without the

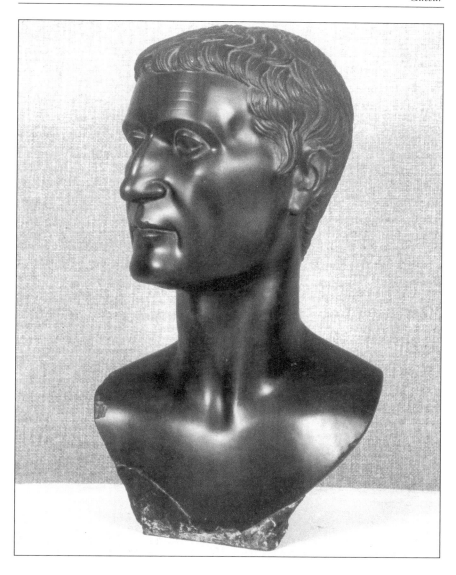

3. *Green basalt head of a Roman, possibly Mark Antony. It was found in Egypt and later acquired at auction by William John Bankes in 1828. It is currently on display in the Egyptian Room at Kingston Lacey, Dorset, England. If it is correctly attributed, it is the only portrait of Antony to survive almost entirely unscathed. The head is noble and more ascetic than other portraits of him, though that need not weigh against its identification as Antony, since it may represent the ennobling vision of the sculptor.*

Courtesy National Trust Photographic Library; photo Paul Mulcahy

oppressive and stern attitude that would have ruined his attempts to reconcile opposing factions. He travelled the length and breadth of the country visiting the troops. In a letter to Cicero, he revealed that Caesar had ordered him to keep a close watch on the ports to prevent anyone from leaving Italy. There were still several important people who had not yet joined Pompey, so it was important for Caesar to retain the moral upper hand, and it was especially important to dissuade people from taking money and materials to Pompey. Antony's education had equipped him for persuasive letter writing; he tried quite eloquently to win Cicero over to the Caesarian cause, by alternately cajoling and then by making veiled threats about what might happen if he decided to join the Pompeians. In the end, Cicero did leave Italy, but his initial vacillation probably did not impress Pompey very much.

Much later, after Caesar's assassination, Cicero tried to blacken Antony's name in connection with his command of Italy during Caesar's absence in Spain. He laid great emphasis in the fact that Antony had ignored the needs of the civilians in the Italian towns while he attended to the troops, and had scandalized the aristocracy of the municipalities by appearing at official receptions in the company of his mistress, an actress no less, and therefore not an asset to the representative of the Roman state. It is significant that even at his most vitriolic Cicero could find nothing more serious with which to charge Antony as Caesar's *magister equitum*. If there had been death and destruction, pillage and looting, or the slightest misdemeanour to report, Cicero would not have wasted his time thinking up fulsome phrases to describe loose morals and actresses. Antony's conduct in Italy may not have been exemplary in so far as his drinking and womanising were concerned, but he would understand the importance of winning over the population of the Italian municipalities, not least because they provided the main recruiting grounds for soldiers and political supporters. The town of Bologna, for instance, provided many of Antony's own political supporters or clients. As he toured Italy, Antony would be constantly aware that he represented not just Rome, but Caesar himself, and he was too level-headed to fail to understand that to offend Caesar would ruin his career. Without Caesar, and Caesar's money and Caesar's support, he would be alone; he would have no hope whatsoever of furthering his political progress by changing his allegiance, since he was by now too much involved with Caesar to make a credible convert to the other side, and in this case there were definitely only two sides to choose from. Antony's family had suffered at the hands of the senatorial party and in particular from the political machinations of Pompey. The thought of throwing in his lot with the Pompeians would probably have made him physically sick. Cicero's accusation that Antony shirked his duties at this time cannot be substantiated; it would have been foolish in the extreme to have neglected any groups of people in Italy who could have formed a large

4.   *Bust of Cicero, Antony's mortal enemy*

        Wellington Museum, London. Photo courtesy of the Victoria and Albert Museum

clientship for Caesar, or for Antony himself.

As well as successes for Antony there were also losses. His friend Curio had been sent to Sicily, and from there he had crossed to Africa with two legions to fight the Pompeians who had allied with Juba, king of Numidia. The expedition was a complete disaster, and Curio was killed. Fulvia was therefore a widow for the second time. In the east, Antony's brother Gaius was captured by the Pompeians, and remained a prisoner until after the final battle at Pharsalus. His troops were recruited into Pompey's army. Nearer home, Caesar had to deal with a mutiny among his own army. The soldiers had fought in Spain and on the way home they had taken Massilia, which had stood against Caesar. They had made some profit from this exercise, but now they were tired and had little to show for all their efforts. Caesar singled out the IX legion and threatened to decimate it, which entailed lining up the soldiers and killing every tenth man. He then made it clear that he would discharge all the rest of the troops, because of course if they were exhausted then they were unfit for service. He addressed them as citizens, not soldiers, as though dismissal were an accomplished fact. In calling their bluff Caesar rapidly brought them to their senses; very soon they were clamouring to fight wherever he sent them. Caesar tidied up by arresting a few ringleaders and executing them.

Politically Caesar was now supreme. Lepidus as urban praetor proposed that Caesar should be made Dictator, an office that was normally called into being in emergencies and held for a temporary period, usually six months. In this instance Caesar's tenure of the post was even shorter than the normal period, since he laid down the Dictatorship and left Rome after only 11 days in the city, having first secured his election as consul for 48, with Servilius Isauricus as colleague. By the time he entered upon his consulship, he was on his way to Greece. There was little time to lose, since Pompey had been recruiting and training his army for a year. Caesar's greatest problem was his lack of ships. He set sail with seven legions and the cavalry, leaving five legions to be ferried across the Adriatic, with Antony in charge of the proceedings. Caesar planned to send his transports back for the rest of his army, but some of them were destroyed. Bibulus, his erstwhile and embittered consular colleague, was in command of the Pompeian fleet, and enjoyed a moment of triumph when he managed to cut Caesar off from the rest of his army. But Caesar proved himself as resourceful as ever. He landed near Palaeste, and soon won over Oricum and Apollonia, where he made camp. He sent messages to Antony to embark the five legions as soon as possible and sail to Oricum, and while in his perilous position, with only half his army holding onto a narrow strip of territory, he sent envoys to Pompey with proposals of peace, but was rebuffed. When Antony did not appear, he tried to set sail in an open boat to cross the Adriatic and hurry the troops along, but the weather and tides conspired against him, forcing him back to land. This story as told by Caesar himself puts a rather more heroic interpretation on the event; he encouraged the captain of the ship with the famous phrase 'Have no fear, you carry Caesar and his fortune'. This time, however, Fortune failed him, and he had to rely on Antony's ingenuity instead.

Antony was experiencing frustrating delays, blockaded in Brundisium by squadrons of the Pompeian fleet under the command of Libo, who occupied the island of Santa Andraea as a base. This was a very strong position for the fleet, but the one commodity that the Pompeians lacked was fresh water. Antony accordingly guarded all the landing places where the Pompeians might come in for water, and waited. Libo was eventually forced to withdraw, and Antony seized his chance. He tried to make for Apollonia, but the wind was in the wrong direction, and forced him towards Nymphaeum, north of Dyrrachium. He made a good landing, skilfully avoiding the Pompeian fleet, and while he was hurriedly disembarking his troops, the wind changed, blowing the enemy ships onto the shore, where they lost several vessels. Antony lost no time in setting off southwards to join Caesar, while at the same time Pompey marched north to intercept him. The potential trap did not work; either Caesarian troops reached Antony to warn him, or he sent out reliable scouts who discovered the Pompeian army. Forethought and knowledge of the enemy plans saved Antony from ambush. It was now Pompey himself who had to give up the pursuit and make his escape, since he was between two armies, having lost the opportunity of eliminating one of them. A heroic stand was out of the question. Pompey withdrew to fight elsewhere.

If Caesar had harboured any doubts about Antony, they ought to have been dispelled after these episodes, which demonstrated that in Antony Caesar had a capable and reliable lieutenant, who would do as he was asked to the best of his ability, and who displayed courage and considerable intelligence in carrying out his orders. Antony had used guile, patience, and his knowledge of geography to outwit Libo, instead of tackling him head on, inviting a battle, and probably losing ships and men in the process. He had embarked as soon as Libo moved off, and after landing at Nymphaeum he had managed to avoid walking straight into Pompey's ambush. Mark Antony, for all his love of wine, women and song, and his dissolute behaviour, had a level head and knew when to remain patiently inactive as well as when to burst into action.

Reunited with Antony, Caesar marched off. As soon as Pompey realised where he was heading, he followed in hot pursuit, so the two armies raced for Dyrrachium. Caesar reached the destination first, but Pompey seized the high ground of Petra. Caesar dug in around the enemy camp, blockading it on three sides with siege works. The result was stalemate, and the campaign now hinged on supplies. Pompey was surrounded, but his troops could be supplied by sea; Caesar on the other hand was free to come and go, but his troops steadily ate their way through the available food and had to go further and further away to find supplies. The situation was compounded by the fact that the Pompeian army had already stripped the immediate territory of most of its available food before Caesar arrived from his war in Spain.

There were two possible solutions. One was to risk everything on a pitched battle, but Pompey wisely avoided committing himself, so Caesar could not bring him to anything more than a minor skirmish. The second solution was simply to wait. Time would tip the balance, for two reasons. Firstly, in the fertile plains at Caesar's back, the crops would eventually grow again, enabling him to feed both men and horses. Secondly, though Pompey could feed his troops on seabourne supplies, he had no fodder for his horses, so it would eventually be Pompey, not Caesar, who found himself in serious difficulties. It was in Caesar's interests to wait and try somehow to survive the starvation of the first months. Before the waiting game bore fruit, Pompey tried to break out. A plan to lure Caesar into a trap was foiled by hard fighting. Next, Pompey attacked the weakest point in Caesar's lines, at the south end near the sea. At this point, Caesar had constructed two lines of defences, one facing inwards to complete the siege works, and one facing outwards to guard against the possibility of ferrying men by sea to outflank the siege lines, thus launching an attack from behind. The theory was sound, but the lines simply extended down to the sea, and had not yet been closed off with a trench and palisade joining the two parallel defences together. It was possible, therefore, to penetrate between the two lines from the coast. Two Gallic chieftains, deserting from Caesar for reasons unknown, gave Pompey all the information he needed to exploit this weak spot. There was an added advantage in that Caesar's main camp was at the extreme northern end of the siege works, while the southern tip was guarded by the quaestor Lentulus Marcellinus, who was ill.

Pompey's attack began in the middle of the night. He ferried 60 cohorts to the point of attack, complete with ladders and light artillery. He had ordered the men to put wicker shields on their helmets to protect them from missiles thrown by the Caesarian troops. He coordinated the attack from the sea with another from within the Pompeian camp, so the Caesarians found themselves in a desperate position, with the enemy to the front and rear, and also between the two lines. The Caesarians broke and ran. Marcellinus' cohorts were unable to reverse the position, but Antony came up from the outposts with 12 cohorts and managed to stabilize the lines. This was no mean feat. If Caesar did not exaggerate wildly, then Antony was outnumbered 4 to 1, and had to instil confidence in men who were badly frightened and had given up. But he did it, somehow. By now he would be a well-known figure, with a reputation for courage and ingenuity. Men would trust him to be able to do something in adverse situations like this. Had they not done so, or had no faith in him, they would have carried on running away. Eventually Caesar himself arrived, hurrying down from the northern sector, and the Pompeians were beaten off.

Pompey's next move was to camp near the siege works, a short distance from the sea, where he could provision his troops and also provide much needed fodder for his horses. Caesar tried to storm the camp in a surprise attack, but failed and once again the Caesarians were routed. If Pompey had followed up this victory immediately it is doubtful if Caesar would have survived; even in the absence of a vigorous pursuit, Caesar decided to raise the siege. He did so in progressive stages. First the baggage, then most of the army left, except for two legions. Caesar intended to keep Pompey guessing until he could get most of the army away; at the last moment, Caesar departed for Apollonia, where he lodged the wounded men. Pompey followed, usually not quite as rapidly as Caesar moved. After it became clear that this was a definite withdrawal and not a short promenade, Pompey was further delayed because his troops had not brought all their baggage with them, and went back to the camp at Dyrrachium for their belongings.

The two armies came to a halt near Pharsalus, where they both made camp. Each day Caesar drew up his army in battle order, but could not tempt Pompey to risk a fight. He decided to march. On the day appointed for breaking camp, Caesar rapidly changed his plans, because on that very day Pompey came out in style. Thus the battle of Pharsalus began. Antony commanded the left wing, with two legions, the Eighth and the Ninth, but they were depleted by their losses at Dyrrachium and their actual strength only amounted to one legion. The decisive action of the battle was on Caesar's right, where he had shrewdly placed eight cohorts of his normal reserve. He brought them into the battle just at the right moment, as the Pompeian cavalry drove the Caesarian horsemen back, exposing the whole of the right wing to attack. The reserve stood their ground with their spears stuck into the earth to form a bristling defensive line. Gradually the tables were turned, and it was the Pompeian left flank which was exposed to attack, but Pompey's troops did not hold their positions. Long before it was over Pompey left the field, because he knew that all was lost. He rode back to camp, then almost immediately left it in unseemly haste, disguised as a trader or a slave, just as the Caesarians broke in. Antony was given the task of pursuing the fleeing Pompeian army, which he did with relentless efficiency. It was an important task, and contributed to the completeness of the victory; too many stragglers left to their own devices could reunite, and become a dangerous element, fighting on in the name of Pompey, or Rome, or the Republic. Caesar needed to eradicate or capture as many as he could.

Unfortunately he did not capture Pompey himself, and on learning that his enemy had gone to Egypt, he followed, because there Pompey could rely upon his connections with Ptolemy Auletes, borrow money and recruit another army, and continue the war. The theory was sound and Caesar could not let it happen; he could not know at this point that Pompey would meet death at the hands of the Egyptian courtiers. One of his immediate and most pressing requirements was for someone with authority to look after affairs in Rome while he himself followed Pompey wherever he went; for this task he chose Antony, who was still his *magister equitum*. As such Antony had access to troops, which emphasised the fact that he was Caesar's lieutenant in more ways than one. Politically Antony was not yet very experienced, but that did not matter very much since it was Caesar who was undoubted master of Rome. Though Antony was the man on the spot, possessing the immediate physical power and authority to make things happen or not happen in the city, no-one could possibly forget that behind him was Caesar, and so they would look far beyond Antony to the time when Caesar returned, for all sorts of reasons, good and bad. It was a time of great uncertainty, when people were unsure of the future in general and their place in the scheme of things in particular. Opportunists and men with grievances stirred up troubles for their own benefit. The first to do so was Marcus Caelius Rufus, whose main cause for unhappiness was that as praetor and a supporter of Caesar he had not been promoted to the more important post of urban praetor, so he bore a grudge which found its expression in his making common cause with the many debtors of Rome. The consul Servilius removed him from Rome, but then he joined forces with Milo in Campania. The latter had returned illegally from exile in Marseilles. The two rebels eventually met their ends separately in different parts of Italy, but it was a precedent for worse things to come, in the city itself, where unrest was fomenting.

Antony began to wear the costume of a general, especially the purple cloak, and he wore his armour and sword even when calling the Senate together, which upset several people. He added insult to injury by going about with a military bodyguard, and six lictors to precede him wherever he went. He took over Pompey's house in Rome and spared no expense in indulging himself and his friends, but seemingly he did not actually pay for the property or its contents. Cicero accused him of going through those contents in a matter of weeks. Antony's lifestyle, flamboyant, ostentatious, not to mention licentious and occasionally debauched, naturally attracted opprobrium. His roisterous reputation is probably not simply a product of retrospective vituperation from Cicero's *Philippics*: Antony always knew how to enjoy life to the full. No-one could ever accuse him of either abstemiousness or discretion. He had a generous nature, and was careless of the consequences of his actions in private life. He lived as he wished to live, and was not scrupulous about his choice of associates — in this he was very different from Caesar, who knew how to be liberal and magnanimous, but at the same time quite decidedly kept his distance from potentially detrimental colleagues. Antony could have learned this much from Caesar, and even more from his rival and eventual enemy, Caesar's great nephew Octavius, who knew that there was no dividing line between public and private life, and who played the part of statesman at all times, even with his closest friends.

The rift between Antony and the Senate was already crystallizing, and it solidified when trouble broke out in earnest, stirred up by Dolabella who made common cause with the many debtors in Rome. Whipped up to desperate fury, these men occupied the Forum, clamouring for the cancellation of debts. The Senate in alarm authorised Antony to restore order. Wisely, Antony had waited until he was asked to intervene, most likely so that if he was castigated for his actions he could fall back on senatorial decree instead of his own initiative as the prime motive. If that was the reason for his delay, it did him no good. He brought his troops to the Forum and surrounded the crowd, possibly hoping that the very presence of soldiers would bring the rioters to their senses. But serious problems arose when the skirmishing escalated into battle, and deaths followed. It is not totally fair to blame all this on Antony. He had started, so he had to finish, and once he realised that he would not be able to clear the Forum without a bloody struggle, he could not use half measures. Naturally the Senate reacted with shocked disapproval and would not back him up. It was even speculated that Antony had been driven on by jealousy and personal rivalry with Dolabella, because the latter had seduced his wife, Antonia. The accusation against Dolabella may be true, especially since Antony divorced Antonia at about this time. These are the bare facts, but it is not certain that jealous rage is the correct interpretation of Antony's actions — it is more likely that there was a great deal of speculation and bending of the facts to fit the theory. The supposition that Antony allowed himself to be ruled by his emotions is not substantiated. He was consistently efficient in a crisis, and perhaps in this case he was simply too efficient. It was an unfortunate circumstance and the result was that, when Caesar returned home, Antony found himself in disgrace, or at least he had to lie low for a while. He received no offices or posts for 46. Lepidus was made consul as Caesar's colleague, and when he left for Africa to pursue the war against the Pompeians, Caesar did not take Antony with him, choosing Dolabella instead. This must have been hard for Antony to contemplate, since it was Dolabella who had caused all the trouble in the first place, and here he was being rewarded with a post in Caesar's entourage and taken on campaign, while the man who had put a stop to the riots languished in Rome, without official appointment, and blatantly out of favour. Caesar could not afford to condone his heavy-handed way of restoring order, even if that had not been Antony's original intention, so for political reasons Caesar dropped him for a while. Most of all Antony had to be seen to pay for Pompey's house and treasures, however much he may have contributed to the defeat of the original owner. Pompey was Caesar's enemy, but he had been a great man, the foremost Roman of his day, and it simply would not be fitting to allow the erstwhile *magister equitum* to take over his belongings in the city. Spoils of war were all very well on the battlefield, but there must be some higher standard of behaviour in Rome.

While Caesar was absent, fighting the African war that was ended by the victory of Thapsus on 6 April 46, Antony was unemployed. He remained so throughout the year, even in September when Caesar celebrated his famous triumphs, four in a row, over Gaul, Egypt, Pharnaces of Pontus and lastly Juba of Mauretania. The final triumph was really over Romans, but Juba had joined the Pompeians, and had lost his life in the conflict, thereby providing the excuse for a triumph over a foreign enemy. The small son of the king of Mauretania, also called Juba, was paraded through the streets, but then spared the execution that usually followed such a spectacle. He was brought up and educated in Rome, and eventually restored to the throne of Mauretania by Augustus, who married him off to Cleopatra Selene, the daughter of Antony and Cleopatra. The same clemency was extended to Arsinoe, the sister of Cleopatra, and Caesar's enemy in the Alexandrian war. After displaying her to the Roman people in his triumph over Egypt, Caesar sent her to Ephesus, but she did not long survive there. In 41 on the orders of Antony and Cleopatra she was put to death.

During the last years of the civil wars against the sons and followers of Pompey, fought in Africa and Spain, Cleopatra was in Rome as the guest of Caesar. She was lodged, notoriously, in his villa across the Tiber. She and Antony must have met at least on a few occasions, but no tradition has survived of their association during these years. Antony may have noticed her, but since she was clearly attached to Caesar, either emotionally or perhaps merely politically, he may have prudently stood back from what was ostensibly denied to him. He was free to seduce the rest of Rome, and perhaps warily avoided becoming too closely involved with anything in Caesar's province. On the other hand he may have been too distracted to notice Cleopatra at all. He remarried at some unknown date, this time choosing the widow of Clodius and of Curio, the lady of fearsome reputation known as Fulvia. He was devoted to her, as all surviving sources attest, even the hostile ones. Antony's enemies used his indulgent affection for Fulvia as evidence of his undignified and extremely un-Roman behaviour. Fulvia was an intelligent and forceful woman, whose activities were decidedly not confined to spinning, weaving and keeping the keys to the larder. She was ambitious, but being female she was forced to achieve her ambitions through and on behalf of her various husbands, the first of whom were disreputable friends of Antony who did not rise very far in the senatorial hierarchy. Married to Antony, Fulvia found a new lease of life and an outlet for her restless ambitions, which of necessity included meddling in politics and military affairs. The fact that she was not brought to heel was construed as a dreadful fault and laid firmly Antony's door. It was said that it was Fulvia who tamed him and accustomed him to obey the orders of a woman. All of this was dreamed up and appropriately applied after he and Cleopatra had begun to represent a serious threat to Octavian, who persuaded the Senate and people that the Egyptian Queen was also a serious threat to Rome itself.

Caesar worked rapidly in Rome, pushing through reforms which he considered necessary, without the attendant freedom of debate that was customary in the Senate. He was made Dictator for the third time, this time for ten years, with specific responsibility for reforming the Republic. One of his most far-reaching reforms was the reorganisation of the calendar, for which task he employed an astronomer from Egypt called Sosigenes, whose calculations were based on a solar year of 365 days, with an extra day to be inserted every fourth year. It was a vast improvement on the old Roman lunar year which required constant adjustment. During the wars, these adjustments had been neglected, with the result that the seasons no longer matched the months to which they were supposed to belong. In order to bring the seasons into line Caesar inserted several more days into the calendar during November. There was little time to attend to the many political affairs that demanded reform, since Labienus and the sons of Pompey had established themselves in Spain and could not be allowed to gain more armed strength or political sympathy. Antony was not given a post with the Caesarian army. Lepidus was made *magister equitum*, and Caesar's great nephew Octavius, too ill to accompany the main entourage, followed on his own initiative with a few of his friends, arriving too late for the decisive battle of Munda on 17 March 45, but nonetheless risking death and destruction on the way. It required ingenuity and courage to travel to a war zone without an army. His actions impressed Caesar, and may have been influential in persuading the Dictator to include Octavius in his will, which he wrote at one of his villas outside Rome before entering the city in yet another triumph. It is said that these details concerning Octavius were added in an appendix, and may not therefore have been part of the original text. The whole problem of Caesar's will is much disputed, but until this time Octavius had not had very much opportunity to demonstrate to his great-uncle that he possessed intelligence and staying power. He went everywhere with Caesar while he journeyed through Spain, settling boundaries, adjudicating between various peoples, receiving embassies. One of these embassies, from Saguntum, came to Octavius himself, believing that he could influence Caesar and bring about a favourable result for the Saguntines, which of course he did, to the great delight of the early biographers of Augustus. Octavius was a discreet youth, shrewd and

5.   *Head of Cleopatra, unadorned but not lifeless. The face is carved with certain
     idiosyncratic features, which suggests that it is an accurate portrayal, and supports
     the opinion of the ancient authors that Cleopatra was not beautiful in the classic
     sense, but wielded considerable charms via her bearing and her voice.*

     © *British Museum*

level-headed, who knew when to talk and when to remain silent. There could be no greater antithesis to Antony, full of life, indiscreet, probably noisy when he should have been quiet, silent when he should have been saying something. The normally taciturn youth Octavius travelled in Caesar's carriage on the way back from Spain, and the two would have ample opportunity to converse and to get to know each other.

On Caesar's return from the wars, overland via the north of Italy, Antony set off to meet him, but when he reached Narbonne, he heard a rumour that Caesar was dead, so he hurried back to Rome. This is the context of the practical joke that he played on Fulvia when he arrived home. He entered the house in disguise, pretending to be his own messenger with a letter from Antony to his wife, declaring his undying love for her. While she read the letter, the false messenger lingered to witness her reaction, which was entirely satisfactory, tearful and quite romantic, belying the usual descriptions of Fulvia as a virago with no redeeming features. At this point Antony threw off his disguise, embraced his wife and presumably lived happily ever after. Plutarch included the anecdote in his biography in order to illustrate Antony's character. One may be permitted to ask what Antony would have done if Fulvia had tossed the letter aside with disdain, but it is not likely that he would have made a mistake of that sort. In general he was an excellent judge of character; his fault was not in evaluation, but in eradication of unsuitable elements.

The rumour that Caesar was dead was of course unfounded, so Antony set off again with Gaius Trebonius to meet his erstwhile chief. This time he was forgiven for his past transgressions; he travelled back through Italy in Caesar's own carriage, relegating Octavius to a second carriage. No-one could be in any doubt that Antony was back in favour. He was promised the consulship with Caesar as colleague for 44. He was 39 years old, and his political career, hitherto sporadically advanced and delayed, was just about to start. He could not possibly have envisaged exactly how. He probably dreamed of army commands under Caesar, a second consulship, a proconsular command of his own, perhaps even eventually stepping into Caesar's shoes as virtual head of state. He probably thought it would take a few years and some hard work. He could not have predicted at this point in his life that in less than six months a cataclysmic series of events would cut short his apprenticeship and propel him to the summit in just two days.

In Rome Caesar took up the reins again. The tribune Lucius Antonius, Antony's brother, arranged a plebiscite in 44 to empower Caesar to nominate the consuls for the following years. Aulus Hirtius and Vibius Pansa were to be consuls for 43, and Decimus Brutus and Lucius Munatius Plancus for 42. These two were to be governors of Gaul before they took up their consular office, Brutus in the Cisalpine province and Plancus in Transalpine Gaul. The other western provinces were also to be handed to Caesarian adherents; Lepidus was to give up office as *magister equitum* and instead to become governor of Nearer Spain and southern Gaul, and Asinius Pollio was to take over command of Further Spain. One man did not receive what he thought his due reward; Gaius Cassius Longinus had been quaestor to Crassus in Parthia, and had done much to re-establish the Roman position in the east after the great disaster. He could normally have expected some important office to mark his political progress, but he was given only a praetorship for 44. He thought he was worth more, and he began to think that all promotion was blocked by Caesar. Such men are dangerous.

Antony did not always bend spinelessly to Caesar's will. As Dictator, Caesar perhaps considered his consulship — it was his fifth — somewhat superfluous, so he resigned it after a short time intending that Dolabella should become consul in his place. It would give him the necessary experience and relieve Caesar of some mundane business, but Antony objected to Dolabella at all times, so he attacked him in a speech in the Senate, precipitating an acrimonious debate. Caesar walked out in disgust. Antony then fell back on his priestly office as augur, declaring the signs unfavourable so that Dolabella could not legally be appointed consul. Finally he got his own way, and succeeded in preventing Dolabella from becoming consul. Caesar seemingly did not bear any grudge against Antony, but Dolabella did.

Grudges were building up against Caesar as the year progressed. Perhaps he knew, but ignored them, since in reality only a fraction of the Senate and people had any serious quarrel with him, and their quarrel was in the main a personal one, however much they dressed it up as a fight for political liberty. It has been pointed out, cynically but accurately, that to the senators liberty meant for the most part the freedom to dominate and exploit the lower classes in Rome and the peoples of the provinces. The Roman system of government had to change to accommodate the development of the Empire. Caesar could see only too clearly what was needed, but he was no longer young and felt that he must hurry. It was his lack of time and consequently his lack of patience that led to his downfall. It was not the changes *per se* that caused all the trouble, for many of his measures were helpful and based on common-sense; rather it was the way in which he went about introducing the changes that he wished to make. It seemed to more and more people that he had no feeling for the old Roman customs, riding rough-shod over them, and sometimes even mocking them. He said that the Republic was just a name, which was eminently true, but anathema to the ears of the patriotically proud Romans who saw no further than the city and subservient peoples around it. He also said that Sulla must have been an idiot to lay down his Dictatorship, which went deep into the consciousness of those who had perhaps hoped that the domination of Caesar would eventually come to an end, and had consequently been prepared to sit it out and wait.

Honours accumulated, granted to him by a Senate that increasingly owed its own status to his power. He had increased the number of senators and filled the House with his own adherents, not all of them of traditional senatorial backgrounds, some of them not even thoroughbred Romans. He enfranchised the Cisalpine Gauls, in an effort to broaden the base of the expanding Roman Empire, extending citizenship to the peoples who formed the Empire and could bring a vital contribution to its growth. There was current joke in the city that no-one would show these new senators the way to the Senate House. The dilution of Roman stock was keenly felt, but what was worse was the knowledge that in his deliberate policy of clemency Caesar held all Rome in his power. He even had a shrine set up to his *Clementia*; he was declared divine himself and Antony was appointed as priest of his cult. Much controversy and debate has been worked out on paper as to the precise meaning of this. Some scholars argue that this divinity was one of the most offensive aspects of Caesar's domination; others more reasonably suggest that the Roman mentality could accommodate divine heroes once they were dead, and that it was never the intention to make Caesar a living god on earth. According to this theory, Caesar was a kind of god in waiting, to be included in the Roman panoply once he had died. It makes sense, in that Antony took up his office as priest of Caesar's cult only many years later, long after Caesar's death, when Antony and Octavian divided the world between themselves.

If there had been anybody left in Rome who thought that once Caesar had achieved all his aims he would then lay down his powers, these men must have been very disappointed when the Dictator accepted the office for life on 14 February 44. The fuss about whether he intended to make himself king ought to have receded in importance after this, but it was still a constant theme, which Caesar perhaps decided to bring to a close next day at the festival of the Lupercalia. This was a very ancient and hallowed fertility ritual that dated far back to Rome's past. Antony's part in this particular festival in February 44 was politically motivated, but to what specific purpose is not known. The motives of the various participants has been debated ever since the event, with no unequivocal result. No-one knows what was in anyone's mind at the time nor why they acted as they did. The festival began, Antony as priest ran the circuit of Rome in the traditional manner, that is clothed in only a loincloth, and then approached the chair where Caesar sat to preside over the proceedings. Somewhere on his dash through the city Antony had picked up a diadem which he offered to Caesar, who refused it. The crowd roared approval that he had not accepted it. Antony offered the crown again, Caesar refused it more emphatically, the crowd roared further approval. There are several possible interpretations. Antony may have instigated the whole escapade on his own initiative, either in the hope that Caesar would accept and become king, or in the hope that Caesar would refuse and thereby convince the people and the Senate that he definitely did not want to be king. On the other hand, Caesar may have collaborated with Antony, in an effort to put an end to all speculation that he wanted to be king. If so, he failed. It simply made matters worse and increased speculation and suspicion, even though Caesar dedicated the crown to Jupiter in the great temple on the Capitol, and ordered the scribes to record the fact that he had refused the kingship to be entered in the *Fasti*, the official journal of the state.

Such fastidiousness did not save him. Within a month, the Liberators of the Republic had struck down the man they called tyrant, at a meeting of the Senate on 15 March, more famously known as the Ides of March. The meeting was to be held in Pompey's Theatre, not the Senate House in the Forum. It was customary to hold meetings at venues other than the Senate House, so Caesar need not have any foreboding about this particular meeting. The famous story of the soothsayer is probably known to everyone. 'Beware the Ides of March' is a familiar catchphrase, but of course Caesar spurned the advice. His wife Calpurnia is said to have tried to prevent him from attending the Senate because of a bad dream she had had the night before, but Caesar was never one to take heed of warnings when there was something that he wanted to do. Decimus Brutus came to his house to share his carriage to Pompey's Theatre, perhaps to allay any suspicions, and of course to make sure that Caesar did actually attend the Senate that day. It would have been embarrassing and somewhat distressing for the Liberators if their victim did not appear. They would then have been forced to sit through the session with daggers hidden in their clothes, and then go quietly home and start all over again.

When they reached their destination, Decimus and Caesar may have waited for Antony to arrive, or perhaps he was already there, waiting for Caesar. No-one really knows. Antony had to be dealt with, of course, so that he could not assist Caesar, and because it was not part of the plot to kill him. It is said that Brutus, idealist that he was, argued against the murder of Antony. The Liberators had designated one or perhaps two of their number to prevent Antony from entering the meeting in Caesar's wake. Therefore Decimus Brutus, and perhaps also Gaius Trebonius, distracted Antony for a moment, while Caesar went ahead into the building. The sources are confused as to who did what but, from Antony's point of view outside the meeting house, so far everything was normal. He would be drawn aside for a few meaningless words. He may have noticed a certain nervousness on the part of the men who were addressing him. Then the commotion would be heard from the audience chamber of the Theatre, followed by crowds of senators fleeing for their lives, probably shouting about murder or perhaps not shouting at all, grimly intent on finding their attendants and going home. By this time it is highly likely that Decimus Brutus and Trebonius would have prudently left

6. *Mark Antony is shown bearded and veiled on this silver denarius of 44. The portrait has religious significance. The curved instrument just under his chin is a* lituus, *a horn used sometimes for military purposes, and also as one of the symbols of the augurs. The two galloping horses and the rider wearing a cap are associated with the Games of Apollo, but the full meaning of this representation is not understood. The design is very similar to one of Caesar's coins, issued shortly before this one, showing him also veiled and looking to the right. It may mean that after the Ides of March, Antony was to step into Caesar's shoes, but this is to stretch the evidence further than it will allow.*

© *British Museum*

Antony, so he probably had to find out for himself what had gone on. It is not known whether he went inside and found Caesar's body. The sources state that he fled, disguised as a slave, or at least not blatantly dressed as a senator, and found refuge in a friend's house. Some time later he went home and barricaded the house, prepared for a siege. Caesar was dead. Antony was his closest associate, and also consul, the chief magistrate who only very recently had offered Caesar the crown. It did not matter now whether it was all a ruse, or whether it had been in deadly earnest. The incontrovertible fact was that Antony, of all the men in Rome, could never disassociate himself from Caesar, and therefore he might have been next on the list for assassination. After a while he would begin to reason, send out spies to gather information, strengthen his position, and consider what to do. He had not been dragged into the Theatre and struck down with Caesar. He had been deliberately drawn aside, but not trapped in a corner to be killed after Caesar was dead. In fact he had been allowed to get away. That probably meant that he had not been a primary target for the assassins, whoever they were, and the fact that no-one was battering his door down some hours after the deadly deed perhaps meant that even in the aftermath of the assassination, he had not been added to the list of victims, if indeed there was such a list. Information was the most urgent need. Gradually Antony would ascertain that the Liberators were a small number of men headed by Brutus and Cassius, and that they had tried to address the crowds in the name of Liberty, but had been driven off and had established themselves on the Capitol Hill, in some confusion that they had not been received with rapturous applause for their act of liberation. They had no military force to speak of, while Lepidus on the Tiber Island had command of several troops. He sent a message that he was prepared to use them as Antony wished. Antony began to rally. He brought legionaries to the Campus Martius and Lepidus blockaded the Capitol.

It is said that only 60 men were party to the plot, which is a very small proportion of the inflated Senate of 900 men that Caesar had created. The Liberators had lofty ideals but not even the lowliest of plans, save that of killing Caesar. Upright and high-minded to the last, they eschewed the use of force, because that would have been the ultimate paradox, to remove a Dictator they hated and then to replace him with an even more despotic narrow-minded rule. Consequently they made no arrangements for the government of Rome or the provinces, imagining that with the tyrant dead everything would automatically revert to the ideal Republic of old, without a hint of military backing or persuasion of some other kind to encourage law and order. The reaction of the people demonstrated to them the extent to which they were out of touch with reality. Not many Romans had felt the need for Liberty in the idealistic sense that Brutus and Cassius imagined. Caesar had done much to ease the lot of the common people, and the soldiers had little quarrel with him. Only the senators had felt themselves oppressed, but without definite plans for their future they had now delivered themselves to Antony.

Always brilliant, clear-headed, and rational in a crisis, Antony acted quickly once he knew the facts. As consul he convened the Senate for 17 March in the temple of Tellus, which just happened to be near his house and not too far removed from his troops.

3 Civil War: Antony defeated

Before the Senate met on 17 March, Antony worked hard and thoroughly reinforced his position. Control of the Caesarian faction was supremely important, as well as control of the Caesarian troops. He began to find out which members of the Senate and people were his friends and which were real or potential enemies. Lepidus turned out to be an ally. He had already been in contact with Antony, and they cooperated in restoring order in the city. There remained men like Oppius and Balbus, Caesar's freedmen secretaries and financiers, and many other Caesarian politicians, military men and equestrian business magnates. Rome was no doubt full of clandestine activity, as slaves and messengers dashed from house to house, putting Antony in touch with as many of Caesar's partisans as possible. Thereafter it was vital to gather all Caesar's papers, which Antony immediately obtained from the great man's widow Calpurnia, without any need for persuasion. Along with the papers came Caesar's secretary Faberius, friendly to Antony, compliant, and replete with a great deal of valuable knowledge. Money was just as vital, and here the sources are murky, some of them accusing Antony of robbing the treasury of the temple of Ops to the tune of 700 million sesterces. The main Treasury of the state was in the temple of Saturn, which Antony left alone. Another charge made against him was that he confused his own finances with the state's, just as Caesar had done, but in Antony's case it was thought that he had used money that was not legally his own to pay off all his debts. The facts are much too tangled now to make any sense of them. Even at the time it is very likely that there was only an approximate accounting system when Antony accumulated funds, no doubt from every source that was available to him in the circumstances. His expenses would be great; there were soldiers to pay and Caesar's veterans to settle on the land, and some semblance of government had to function even though Rome may have been at a standstill. For a while, Antony *was* the government, and he shouldered the burden extremely well. There was so much to do in a very short time, and he had not wasted a single moment from 15 to 17 March, indeed he had probably scarcely slept since the terrible events in the Theatre of Pompey.

Now on 17 he faced the Senate, not quite an unknown quantity to him since he cannot have failed to sound out various people during the previous day and night. The debate was stormy, but Antony allowed each to have his say. If he had so wished he could have had all Rome under his thumb, lining the streets with soldiers and dictating terms to all and sundry. Instead he took a calculated risk and endeavoured to bring everything as far as possible back into normal working order. Chaos was only a hair's breadth away, but Antony did not wish to impose rigid control, nor was he ready for open warfare just yet. The restoration of law and order was of paramount importance, and an all-embracing amnesty was the only way to bring it about. Cicero proposed such a measure, and it found ready acceptance. There was a tremendous dilemma to be overcome before the state could be put on an even keel. A murder had been committed in full view of Rome, and it was not just a back-street skirmish or a drunken brawl. It was a planned assassination, intended to be conspicuous. The vexed question was how to deal with it. If Caesar was innocent, then the Liberators ought to be punished, which would tear the state apart and precipitate another civil war. On the other hand, if Caesar was guilty, deserving of the name of tyrant, then the Liberators ought to be praised to the skies, and consequently all the Dictator's acts could be annulled. That of course was impossible, as Antony pointed out. Most of the senators owed their positions to Caesar; most of the magistrates both present and future had been appointed by Caesar; most of the current provincial governors were in office because Caesar had put them there. To annul all his acts would be tantamount to abolishing the entire governmental system at one stroke. It followed, therefore, that it would be better to confirm all Caesar's acts, rather than to try to sift through them, confirming some and annulling others. Antony achieved this and more, in that the Senate agreed to confirm all the existing measures, and also those that Caesar had merely intended. That gave Antony a free hand to select from Caesar's papers all those measures that he felt would be advantageous both to the Republic and to himself. His measures were sensible and just; they were not revolutionary, not high-handed, not purely selfish, and nowhere near dictatorial, but nonetheless the result was that people began to doubt the authenticity of what Antony said he had found among the jottings of the Dictator.

Reconciliation was the order of the day for the time being. There was to be no witch-hunt of the murderers of Caesar, no trials or lynchings or civil war. It was a stupendous achievement, given the circumstances, and most Romans were probably agreeably surprised at Antony's firm but just statesmanship. As guarantee for his good faith, Antony sent his infant son to the Capitol as hostage in the camp of the Liberators and, when the Senate had agreed to the amnesty, he and Lepidus entertained the Liberators to dinner, to demonstrate the new concord that reigned in the city. The dinners were probably strained affairs, an interesting amalgam of reconciliation and indigestion in equal measure. But it was the play-acting that counted, not real feelings.

Antony's task was monumental, with all the attributes of an uphill struggle. Personal survival was the first necessity, with sufficient power to ensure that he remained not only alive but in charge. Eventually he gathered together a bodyguard of 6000 men, but mostly as a declaration of intent; he did not put them to any aggressive use. Next he had to reconcile all sorts of disparate entities whose prime motives were alarmingly similar to his own, so he needed to combine precisely balanced amounts of seduction and subjugation, depending on the personages with whom he had to deal at each step of the way. He was no friend of Dolabella, and had blocked his elevation to the rank of consul, but now allowed him to take up the post that Caesar had intended him to hold. The general amnesty had been successfully brought about and the Republic shakily preserved without recourse to arms, but the fine balance that Antony had achieved was about to be permanently disrupted. He may not have recognised the fact just yet. On 18 March the Senate agreed to ratify the terms of Caesar's will. The provisions were quite poignant in that Caesar had left money and valuables to some of the men who had killed him. His gardens were to be opened to the public, and he had left money to every Roman citizen. One quarter of his fortune went to his male relatives, Pedius and Pinarius, to be divided equally between them. Antony was mentioned only in the second rank of legatees, so if he had expected to profit from Caesar's will he was disappointed, but his relegation to second rank does at least vouchsafe for his honesty in not tampering with the will or trying to forge parts of it in his own favour. His lack of financial profit was not the hardest blow, nor his most troublesome problem. By far the greatest part of Caesar's wealth went to Gaius Octavius, his great-nephew, the grandson of his sister Julia. The money by itself would not have enabled the teenaged Octavius to achieve very much, though it certainly assisted him in his bid to step into Caesar's shoes, which he was soon to do. He was in Macedonia when Caesar was assassinated, and on hearing the news he set off immediately to return to Rome, where he arrived probably in May. His inheritance embraced more than just money. At the end of the will there was a clause declaring Caesar's intention that Octavius should be adopted as his son, a clause which has caused many problems to ancient and modern scholars alike, and one which Octavius took very seriously. He began to style himself Gaius Julius Caesar, without even adding Octavianus to his name, as he was entitled to do in order to demonstrate that he had been adopted into the Julian clan from that of Octavius. The name Octavian is now so entrenched in modern accounts that it is unecessarily pedantic to insist on calling him Caesar.

Although adoption of an heir was a regular practice in Rome, it was nearly always carried out while both parties were still alive. It is very doubtful whether testamentary adoption had any real basis in Roman law. Indeed some modern scholars deny that it was legal at all. This may be why Octavian made every effort to have the adoption formally ratified by a law of the people passed in public assembly. Antony made vague offers of help, but while not actively obstructing him he worked behind the scenes to prevent the legalisation of the adoption. Octavian had to abandon the scheme, temporarily. He had no intention of forgetting about it. When he became consul it was his first concern, and the law was duly passed. Octavian firmly intended to take Caesar's place, but he was careful to start out in properly legalised fashion. He could not afford to leave any loopholes for clever politicians to exploit later on in his career.

In March 44 Antony knew nothing of the schemes of Caesar's great-nephew. Once he was sure of his own position, Antony was able to take charge of the funeral arrangements for the murdered Dictator. The ceremony took place on 20 March in the Forum. Antony made a speech, to which Cicero refers, but the contents of the speech are unknown. Both Dio and Appian invent noble words which have no basis in fact, and each of them use the speeches to put across their own points of view. Despite this blatant literary device, Dio and Appian possibly adhere quite closely to the spirit of what Antony actually said. The important event was the reaction of the people, who made it clearer than they had on the Ides of March that they did not greet the removal of the Dictator with joy. The unknown quantity here is the extent to which Antony intended to stir up these feelings, or alternatively how much of the popular demonstration was spontaneous and beyond his control. It is very likely that he engineered it all, in true demagogue fashion, in order to say through other mouths what he probably wanted to say himself. Antony was an emotional man, but when it mattered he kept his emotions under control. If he had given the word, he could have started a war, but he kept his head. He was consul, and responsible for the whole Roman world. But he had been Caesar's friend for a long time. He was closer to the real world than the high-minded Brutus and Cassius, and he knew the feelings of the people. Why should he not use those feelings to demonstrate his own at second-hand?

The Liberators found themselves in very bad odour. Antony made it possible for Brutus and Cassius to remove themselves from Rome, even though strictly speaking they were in office and should not leave the city. As a political gesture which cost him nothing he abolished the Dictatorship. This measure brought him considerable support, even though it did nothing to abolish the harsh fact that whoever possessed the political prestige, the troops, and the patronage of large numbers people, could aspire to a dictatorship no matter what it was actually called. Caesar was dead, but Caesarian politics were still very much alive.

The government of the provinces was among Antony's next concerns. Caesar had made most of the arrangements in advance, but now some fine

7.   *Antony's younger brother Gaius Antonius was sent to Macedonia as governor in 44, when Antony decided to exchange his province for Gaul. This silver denarius of 43 shows the head of a man, possibly Gaius, in Macedonian dress with a cap and a Greek style chlamys, or cloak. The legend proclaims him C. ANTONIUS. M.F. PRO. COS. (Gaius Antonius, son of Marcus, Proconsul). The reverse shows religious symbols and the word pontifex, meaning priest — an office which Gaius held from 45 until his death in 42. He was captured and executed by Brutus before the battle of Philippi.*

© *British Museum*

tuning was necessary. The Senate confirmed the provincial governors in their new posts. Decimus Brutus departed to take up his post as governor of Cisalpine Gaul. Brutus and Cassus had been given interim tasks, namely the charge of the corn supply in Asia and Sicily, to remove them from Rome and enable them to fill in their time profitably before they took up their posts as provincial governors. Dolabella was to be governor of Syria, and Antony was assigned to Macedonia, but that was part of Caesar's plans for the Danube campaign and then the Parthian problem. If Caesar had lived, Antony would have gone to Macedonia after his consulship ended, but now the situation had changed. Parthia had receded in importance, and the arrival in Rome of Octavian, determined to claim his full inheritance at all costs, meant that, whatever political and personal rivalry ensued between any of the parties contending for power, the struggle would centre on Rome. Antony needed a different base nearer the scene of action. He chose Cisalpine Gaul, from which province he could oversee Italy and control what happened there. Accordingly he had a law passed to give him the province and remove Decimus Brutus from it. Octavian assisted him, actively canvassing on his behalf to encourage the people to pass the law. He and Antony worked together, but only because the soldiers had coerced them. Besides, Octavian may have had an ulterior motive, in that he was more interested in removing Decimus, one of Caesar's assassins, than he was in installing Antony as governor of Cisalpine Gaul. The main problem was that Decimus Brutus was not inclined to leave without a fight, so Antony required more troops than were currently at his disposal to persuade Decimus to go. He decided to bring back to Italy four of the five legions that were stationed in Macedonia, in readiness for Caesar's projected campaigns; he left one legion in the province and put his brother Gaius in office as governor. In that way he could control two areas at once, watching both the eastern and western halves of the Roman world.

His plans for his future were sound, but he was hindered by the persistence and determination of Octavian. Whereas Antony had played down the connection with Caesar after all due reverence had been shown at his funeral, and managed to obliterate the name and hopefully some of the memory of the Dictatorship, Octavian blatantly advertised his descent from the Dictator, and seized upon every opportunity to remind people of him. Worse still, he vowed revenge for Caesar's death. Such inflammatory behaviour reversed all that Antony had tried to do to establish peace. When Octavian tried to display Caesar's golden chair at the *Ludi Ceriales*, Antony blocked him. When it was rumoured that Octavian wanted to become tribune in the place of the dead Helvius Cinna, Antony used all his influence to prevent that too. Thwarted on this occasion, thereafter nearly everything played into Octavian's hands. He put on splendid games in honour of Caesar, during which a comet appeared, visible in the night sky for several days. People said it was a sign that Caesar had indeed become a god, just as had been decreed in advance when the living Caesar was declared divine. Octavian naturally found it extremely advantageous to be able to claim descent from a god, and he advertised the fact to greatest effect. Coins appeared depicting the comet, called *sidus Iulium*, the star of Julius Caesar; decorative stars appeared on the statues of Caesar; Octavian eventually began to call himself the son of a god, *divi filius*.

Antony cannot have failed to take note of the proceedings and the power-seeking inclinations of Octavian. He has been accused of failing to take due account of Octavian, and of consistently underestimating him. None of this speculation is sufficiently accurate. Antony may have been reckless in some areas of his life but he was not a fool, and he walked with both feet firmly on the ground. The fact that he tried to curb Octavian's efforts to connect himself with Caesar demonstrates that he realised the dangers of such a connection, but he was scarcely in a position to do more than the law allowed. He possessed considerable power whilst he was consul, but the only certain way of blocking Octavian altogether was to kill him, and Antony was not sufficiently ruthless for that extreme measure. Therefore he had no choice except to try to second-guess Octavian's next move, constantly manoeuvring to stay one step ahead. The sources imply that Antony brought all his later problems on himself by his cavalier treatment of Octavian, who is depicted as the injured party, dealt with roughly by Antony at their first meeting and cheated out of some part of his inheritance because Antony had squandered it. It must be remembered that the sources are not contemporary and the account of Antony's behaviour has been revised in the light of the eventual success of Octavian. Much emphasis is placed on the fact that the poor young man was forced to sell his own property and to beg for financial assistance from his relatives Pedius and Pinarius, in order to pay the people of Rome the sums due to them according to the terms of Caesar's will. Antony was cast as the villain who consciously deprived good Roman citizens of their rights, as well as embarrassing the innocent great-nephew of Caesar. This was part of the psychological game that Octavian was intent on winning. He was much more devious than Antony, and on occasion he outwitted him, which lends spurious support to the theory that Antony underestimated him. Antony neither underestimated Octavian nor overestimated his own abilities, but he suffered from the scandalous reputation that had already become embedded in perceptions of him, whereas Octavian at the age of 19 was an unknown quantity. He was therefore free to establish a carefully scripted reputation for himself, mostly favourable at the time and quite definitely revised and rewritten after the civil wars. When Antony tried his hand at the psychological game, claiming that Octavian had infiltrated his bodyguard with the intention of having him assassinated, he gained no sympathy at all. No-one really believed him, and quite a few men possibly wished that Octavian had succeeded. The truth will never be known. Antony may have made it all up to discredit Octavian, but on the other hand the ruthless young man may well have decided that he really needed to remove his main rival. It has been pointed out that the two of them had more to gain by forming an alliance, but that was later, when other parties had been eliminated.

Gradually, as a result of the devious activities of Octavian, closely followed by the vituperative speeches and machinations of Cicero, Antony found himself out of favour with too many influential people. After the Ides of March Cicero had avoided the political scene, but he had been in contact with Octavian since the young man had arrived in Italy. In the autumn, having stood on the sidelines for several months, he saw his chance to save the state, repeating the heroic stance of his consulship nearly 20 years earlier. Antony summoned the Senate for 1 September, but Cicero failed to attend. The meeting was arranged in order to confer upon Caesar religious honours that far exceeded anything yet seen for an ordinary mortal. At the meeting of the Senate held on the following day, Cicero said that he had not attended because he could not condone such honours. Then he launched into the first of the diatribes now known as the *Philippics*, in which he consistently cast Antony as the foremost enemy of the state. During this first speech, Antony was not present, but naturally he heard of it and the story presumably lost nothing in the retelling. It took 17 days for Antony to respond in kind, but his speech is not recorded. He was probably quite stunned by this attack on him. His personal quarrel with Cicero on behalf of his step-father Lentulus had never coloured his relationship with the orator in any of his political dealings up to now. The resentment was most likely still festering in the background, but Antony had not allowed it to surface even in private correspondence. The letters that survive from Antony, reproduced in Cicero's own letters, are polite, reasonable, even deferential. The animosity that sprang up fully fledged is purely Cicero's, not Antony's, so the tirade presumably came as an unexpected blow to Antony. The Roman political scene was not a suitable one for wilting wallflowers, but Cicero's speech was, in modern parlance, right over the top, and bewilderingly inappropriate as well as unfair. After striving to bring concord to the state, and indeed achieving and maintaining an admittedly fragile peace without setting himself up as an autocrat, Antony had been painted in the darkest colours as the greatest enemy of Rome since Hannibal. Like any reasonable politician with a sense of reality, he would have expected opposition, because he had encouraged freedom of speech, but when he heard of the gross accusations of Cicero he may have wished momentarily that he had taken over the city and gagged everyone while he had the chance.

The war of words went on for a short time, while Octavian steadily consolidated his position. He raised troops from among Caesar's veterans, without authority to do so. His excuse for this illegality was that he was protecting himself from Antony. He and Cicero were beginning to sound the same call to arms, each for their own purposes. Cicero desperately wanted to play the part of saviour, and would twist any fact to be able to do so. Octavian wanted legitimate power to enable him to avenge Caesar, and that meant, ultimately, supreme power. It was only a matter of time before he and Cicero formed an alliance. The one entity that was lacking was an enemy who posed a serious threat, a deficiency that was soon resolved when it seemed that Antony was intent on emulating Caesar by going to Gaul and from there influencing Roman politics. The senators were sensitive about such things, and now that they allowed themselves to be represented more and more by Cicero, they convinced themselves that they required an army to use against Antony. Octavian had an army but required legal sanction to use it, which only the Senate could give him. What one party lacked, the other could supply. War was now a definite possibility.

Matters came to a head in November. When Antony went to meet his legions arriving from Macedonia, he found that they had been subverted by

Octavian, and their loyalty to him was suspect. These troops had made the acquaintance of Octavian while he was in Apollonia, waiting for Caesar to begin his Danube campaign. They had been raised by Caesar and were prepared to fight for him, but after his death their loyalties will have been divided between the two Caesarian leaders, so it is not surprising that some of the troops wavered. Antony executed about 300 of the ring leaders. It is said that Fulvia was with him, revelling in the bloodshed, but that may be scandalous invention. Antony then paid the loyal troops more than Caesar had left the populace of Rome in his will, but it is said that the soldiers thought it a paltry sum. It is highly likely that Octavian made full use of their vacillation by offering them more money than Antony could afford.

While Antony marched his troops back towards Rome, he was still in control of the government. Octavian and Cicero had not yet concluded their unofficial alliance and Octavian at this juncture was simply an illegal adventurer at the head of troops. Moreover he had just made a serious mistake. Impatient for action, trying to forestall retaliation by Antony, he had marched some of his army to Rome, but had failed to rouse support. He had gone off to the north to lie low for a while. Antony hurried back to Rome, fully intent upon calling the Senate together to declare Octavian a public enemy and outlaw (*hostis*). There was every chance that he might succeed. He had primed his agents, and he had the full weight of the law on his side. Then he abandoned the idea and marched north instead. Two of his Macedonian legions, the Fourth and the Martia, had gone over to Octavian. He gathered the rest, and stopped at Tivoli, where many senators and equestrians came to meet him and swore loyalty to him. The gesture was a spontaneous demonstration, and served to strengthen his resolve. He did not march on Rome, as Cicero had suggested that he might do. For many reasons, Antony withdrew. His consulship was coming to an end in a month's time. He could gain nothing except accumulating problems with no time to resolve them if he went back to Rome, but he knew that there were some senators and equestrians who would support him and look after his interests while he was absent. It was better to continue while the going was good, take what troops were loyal to him and use them to oust Decimus Brutus from Cisalpine Gaul. Once he was established there, he would be in a better position to build up his influence in Italy. A more hot-headed commander might have succumbed to anger, and gone straight to Rome on a vengeful quest. But Antony was not ready for that and was too level-headed to contemplate it. Arriving in Rome would have been difficult enough, but maintaining a hold on it would have been even harder. Such a project required careful planning, involving either an assiduous, prolonged cultivation of supporters, or alternatively a very thorough and rapid elimination of enemies. When Antony did come back to Rome, accompanied by two colleagues, he chose the latter.

Antony proceeded to Rimini, on the border between Italy and Cisapline Gaul. As the legally appointed governor of the province, he cordially invited Decimus Brutus to leave it. The Senate, on the other hand ordered Decimus to stay where he was. In effect, this meant that the Senate had refused to recognise Antony, thus placing him in an anomalous position. He could not return to Rome, and if he succeeded in removing Decimus Brutus he would be committing an illegal act in the eyes of the Senate. There was every reason for Antony to establish himself rapidly in command of the province. Decimus had fewer troops and so did not put up much of a fight. He was quickly bottled up in Mutina (modern Modena), where he prepared for a siege. Antony obliged. He needed quick results if he was to avoid having to fight on two fronts. The new consuls would take up office on 1 January 43, and it was highly probable that the Senate would instruct them to assist Decimus. Cicero was already making himself the saviour of the state, and had begun to canvass for support for Octavian. As soon as the new consular year was inaugurated, he set about extracting recognition from the Senate for the young commander and his army, and there could be only one reason for doing so. Very soon Antony would find himself at war, sandwiched between Decimus' troops blockaded in Mutina, and the relieving armies of Octavian and the consuls.

The alliance with Cicero was profitable for Octavian. He was presented to the Roman world not as a calculating opportunist bent on self-preservation and revenge for Caesar's death, but as the boy-hero whose timely action had saved the state from Antony. Cicero persuaded the Senate to elevate Octavian to senatorial status, together with the rank of propraetor with full powers, which would give him the necessary powers and legal basis (*imperium*) to command an army. In addition Octavian was to be regarded as having already held the quaestorship, the important point being that he would therefore be allowed to stand for election to any office that normally followed the quaestorship. This was all passed by the Senate in blatant disregard of the age limits placed upon the tenure of such political offices. Cicero pointed out that youth was not necessarily a disadvantage in political and military circles, and finally he vouched for Octavian's good character. He imagined that he could control the young man, and use him to crush Antony. That one overriding purpose blinded him to the possibility that the teenaged Octavian might have plans of his own. Cicero saw no further than placing the Senate in command of Rome, and restoring the Republic to its ancient glory. When that was achieved, he thought he could discard Octavian.

The new consuls of the year, Hirtius and Pansa, were duly allotted the task of assisting Decimus Brutus, and Octavian was assigned to the same task. The war of Mutina had almost begun, but Antony still had friends in the Senate. Lucius Calpurnius Piso and Quintus Fufius Calenus spoke for him, trying to avoid war by suggesting that an embassy should be sent to Antony, to ask him to give up Cisalpine Gaul. His reply was perfectly reasonable: he would leave Cisalpine Gaul if he could go to Transalpine Gaul, to hold it for five years. He also requested, quite legitimately, that all his acts as consul should be ratified. He could hardly have expected that these requests would be granted, since he can have had no illusions now about Cicero's implacable hostility, nor about his persuasive powers in the Senate.

Antony showed himself fully aware of all the implications of the alliance between Octavian, Cicero and the Senate. He recognised the weaknesses of such an unlikely association and saw through the different, not to say divergent, ambitions of each of the participants. His reply to a letter from Octavian and Hirtius is preserved in part in the Thirteenth *Philippic*, where Cicero cites passages from it and answers the points raised. It shows that Antony had a firmer grasp of reality than many of the senators who were swayed by Cicero's oratory.

The senatorial army did not unite until spring. Octavian and the consul Hirtius made camp near Bononia (modern Bologna) where they waited for the other consul Pansa to bring up more troops from Rome. They moved closer to Mutina in March, and as they did so Antony abandoned Bononia, strengthened the blockade of Mutina and decided to launch an attack on one army before the two consuls could join forces. His intelligence networks were accurate, and it was a sound strategy to take advantage of the enemy's split forces. It nearly paid off. On 14 April Antony laid an ambush and fell upon Pansa's troops, mostly inexperienced recruits, and routed them. Pansa was wounded, and several days later died of his wound. Unfortunately Antony had no time to consolidate the victory or regroup his army. While the soldiers were still scattered, Hirtius came up to rescue his colleague, putting Antony into a dangerous situation. It is to Antony's great credit that as the evening progressed into night he withdrew in reasonable order. These bloody skirmishes were collectively known as the battle of Forum Gallorum. Octavian's part in it was to defend the camp near Mutina. He shared in the honours granted by the Senate, and along with the two consuls was hailed by the soldiers as Imperator, which was to become the most important title of the Emperors of Rome.

The next battle followed within a few days, near Mutina. The consul Hirtius was killed, but Antony had to acknowledge defeat. He wasted no time in coming to a decision; he abandoned the siege of Mutina, rounded up what was left of his army, and set off to cross the Alps into Gaul. He was not certain of his reception there. During the previous month, it seemed that the other Caesarian governors — Munatius Plancus in Transalpine Gaul, Lepidus in southern Gaul and Nearer Spain, and Pollio in Further Spain — might join him, or at best remain neutral, but times had changed. Antony's defeat had been greeted with near-delirium in Rome. In his previous speeches Cicero

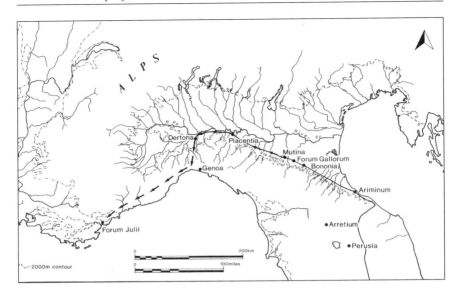

8.   *Map of northern Italy. After the battles of Mutina in April 43, Antony retreated into Gaul by way of Placentia (Piacenza) and Dertona (Tortona), joining up with Ventidius Bassus about thirty miles west of Genoa, and arriving at Forum Julii (Frejus) in May.*

Drawn by Graeme Stobbs

had tried unsuccessfully to have Antony declared an enemy of the state and an outlaw (*hostis*), but the senators had not dared to take matters that far. Now that they thought it was safe they did so with alacrity, overwhelming anyone who tried to speak up for Antony. His defeat was considered decisive. It was thought that Rome had seen the last of him. Thanksgiving to last for 60 days was decreed, and Decimus Brutus was ordered to pursue and annihilate him.

It was time for Antony to take stock of the possibilities open to him. Retreating over the Alps in the cold winds of April, surrounded by a defeated and starving army whose loyalty was sorely tested, cut off from his family who were now outlaws because of senatorial hostility to him, Antony perhaps came to grim terms with fate. After all he had done to keep the state on a even keel, punishing none of the Liberators and exercising every restraint, Rome had rejected him. Very well. There were other places, other armies. He was not beaten yet.

4 Civil War: Antony victorious

Crossing the Alps is not an easy task without modern roads and vehicles, and in April 43 it was particularly difficult. The snows had not melted in the passes and there were no supplies. Antony had not had time to gather rations before he raised the siege of Mutina and withdrew. He could not afford to delay, so the army had to live hand to mouth, content with what it could find on the march, which was precious little. Plutarch tells of Antony drinking brackish water without flinching in order to encourage the men. In a crisis he was always brilliant, sustaining hardships that might have broken other leaders even if there was hope of salvation at the end of the hardships, but in this case there was none. Antony had no guarantee that he would not have to make war to stay alive in Gaul, nor could he be certain that some of his own men might not decide that they had had quite enough of following a loser and suddenly turn against him. He probably reflected that loyalty is a fragile commodity, usually proportionately related to the benefits that ensue from it, and more often than not subordinated to self-interest. He was an outlaw, beyond state protection. He had no legal status and no right to command troops. His death would be welcomed by many, and the person who despatched him would be regarded as a hero. Apart from his own safety there was that of his family in Rome; he perhaps did not know at this stage that Fulvia had found protection with Cicero's great friend and correspondent Atticus, who kept out of politics, did not take sides, extended kindness to all and sundry no matter what their associations, and survived to old age.

It was not all doom and gloom on the march into Gaul, despite the fact that in the mountains there was nothing to eat except tree bark, and no clean water to quench thirst. There were some brighter moments. On 3 May Antony was joined by three new legions raised and led by his friend Ventidius Bassus, who had skilfully avoided any military encounter on his way northwards, and successfully evaded Decimus Brutus' troops which were in pursuit of Antony. Ventidius was an adventurous character who had started life in difficult and humble circumstances. His family had been on the wrong side in the Social War. As a child, Ventidius was taken prisoner and led through the streets of Rome as one of the human trophies in the triumphal procession of Pompeius

Strabo, the father of Pompey the Great. Ventidius rose via the army and attracted the notice of Caesar, whose loyal follower he had been for many years. From Caesar's side he progressed to Antony's, joining him with fresh troops as he retreated into Gaul — more mouths to feed, but heartening because Antony was about to enter the province of Gallia Narbonensis and he now had enough troops to counter anything that the legitimate governor, Marcus Aemilius Lepidus, might do to stop him. But in fact nobody seemed able or willing to stop him, perhaps because Antony's reputation as a soldier went before him, and because potential opponents would reason that here was a man leading troops who, like himself, were experienced, battle-hardened, hungry, angry, and had very little to lose. Lepidus posted a guard at the mouths of the passes, under the command of Culleo, but when Antony's brother Lucius approached with the advance guard on 7 May, Culleo made no effort to block him. By the middle of May Antony and the whole army were in Gaul.

Lepidus faced the most important crossroads of his life. He was one of Caesar's generals, a respected patrician, and Pontifex Maximus thanks to Antony, with whom he had co-operated in the aftermath of the Ides of March. He was a close associate if not a friend of Antony, and probably had no desire at all to fight with him. On the other hand he wished to retain the high regard of the Senate, without which he could not progress to higher things. He was in regular correspondence with the Senate, writing lots of words but actually saying little until he knew how matters would turn out. He could not be certain that Antony would emerge victorious from the low level to which he had been reduced. Lepidus no doubt reasoned that to throw in his lot with an outlaw would probably finish his career and also his life. He had his family to think of as well. Whatever he did would reflect on them.

The Senate, led by Cicero, tried to win him to their cause. Cicero flattered him by voting him a golden statue for his work in coming to an agreement with Sextus Pompey, who was now operating on behalf of the Senate, using his fleet to secure the Mediterranean. The honour of having a statue in the Forum rendered no help to Lepidus in his present circumstances. He stalled for as long as he could, writing anodyne reports, and finally moving his legions to block Antony's progress. Antony was camped on the banks of the river Argenteus, so Lepidus camped on the opposite bank. The soldiers began to fraternise. One day Antony, long-haired and bearded, walked casually into Lepidus' camp. The alliance was forged. Lepidus wrote to the Senate to say that his hand had been forced by his soldiers. Some scholars have doubted the authenticity of the story that Antony walked right up to Lepidus' tent, but the truth about how the alliance came about does not really matter. The tale has a definite Antonian panache about it that found ready acceptance in ancient times. The disregard for personal safety, the all-or-nothing gamble was so typical of Antony. He knew Lepidus' character, and he had tested the temperament of the two armies, so it could be said that he acted upon a safe bet, but nonetheless it took courage to confront Lepidus' troops, ignoring the risk that one of Lepidus' officers might take it upon himself to be a hero and do his commander a favour. It would be small comfort to him to know that his potential assassin would not survive the next few seconds.

The Senate promptly declared Lepidus an outlaw. His own brother Aemilius Paullus instigated the proceedings, possibly to remove himself from all suspicion. Perhaps the senators did not stop to reflect that their actions had just united two of the foremost Caesarian leaders, whose desperate position gave them common cause to use the ten legions which they had at their joint disposal.

Theoretically, Lepidus and Antony were threatened on two fronts. In Transalpine Gaul there was Plancus with three legions, backed up by Pollio in Further Spain with two more legions. From Italy, Decimus Brutus pursued Antony with weary troops who had been severely weakened during the siege and blockade of Mutina. Octavian was ordered to help Decimus, but he stayed put, holding onto his own troops and also those of the dead consul Pansa. Here was a rift to be exploited. Octavian had received no rewards after the Mutina battles, and although it had been solemnly promised that the rewards that he had promised his soldiers would be paid, nothing was forthcoming from the Senate. The committee had been formed to look into the question of the settlement of veterans, but Octavian had not been asked to sit on it, so he could not personally represent his own troops, nor could he protect their interests. On a more personal level, Octavian had been informed that Cicero had spoken about him in public, saying that the young commander should be praised, rewarded, and immortalised. The phrase sounds innocuous enough in English translation, but in Latin it is a clever pun. The word used for 'immortalised' (*tollere*) has two meanings, one denoting elevation to fame, and the other elimation by death. Cicero was a master of words, and could never resist the urge to be clever, especially when he had an audience. He could not dissimulate either, because he still thought that he was in control of Octavian. At the beginning he could not have foreseen that both consuls would be killed in the war against Antony, and he never seemed to grasp the fact that Octavian would never cooperate fully with Decimus Brutus, who had helped to murder Caesar. Either Cicero fatally misjudged, allowing his hatred of Antony to blind him to the purpose that Octavian had set himself, or Octavian himself put on an entirely credible performance so that Cicero believed that he had no other purpose except the elimination of Antony. In truth, all that Octavian required at first was legal command of an army. Now he had set his sights somewhat higher. The consulship was vacant, and Octavian meant to have it. With unassailable political power he would be able to obtain all he wanted — legalisation of his adoption as Caesar's son, condemnation of Caesar's murderers, and sufficient status to face Antony on equal terms.

For about a month, Octavian laid low, pretending that he could not control his troops and that they would not march with Decimus Brutus against Antony. In June he sent a deputation of centurions and soldiers to the Senate, to ask for the consulship for their commander. Inadvisedly, the Senate made a stand, and refused. Octavian no doubt expected that the Senate would do so, but it was all part of the elaborate game to do everything as properly as he could. There was a small chance that he might have obtained the consulship after his soldiers had asked politely for it, in which case he could have taken it up legally without the expenditure of too much effort. After the polite questions, there remained the last resort of force. When it was clear that the Senate would not cooperate with him, Octavian wasted no time in marching on Rome. Only now beginning to panic, the Senate summoned two legions from Africa, and called out the legion of recruits that Pansa had left near Rome, but the senators had left it too late to take any effective action. After a little contretemps when the Senate mistakenly put their faith in a rumour that two of Octavian's legions had deserted him, the senators confronted reality and gave in. Just short of his twentieth birthday, Octavian was elected consul and took up office on 19 August, with his kinsman Pedius as colleague.

Watching from the sidelines in Gaul and Spain, Plancus and Pollio decided that their best policy was to do nothing, biding their time, awaiting the outcome. They knew Antony, and perhaps did not consider him so easy to defeat as the Senate did. Pollio came over to Antony in July, but Plancus wavered a little longer, writing reports to Cicero, expressing surprise and then dismay that Octavian had not marched to help Decimus. Plancus and Decimus joined forces in August, but then Octavian became consul, and so Plancus yielded to the inevitable. He and Pollio were after all Caesar's men, more comfortable with Antony than with the assassins. Decimus' troops guessed correctly what was happening and went over to Antony. Decimus was out on a limb, deserted except for a few officers. He went north to the Rhine, but was killed by a Gallic chief, who probably did as Antony told him, or who knew that Antony would not mind in the least if he received Decimus' head as a present.

The way was now open for an alliance between Antony and Octavian. Correspondence may have been winging its way northwards to Antony from Octavian long before he obtained the consulship. This is one of history's imponderables, but it can be assumed that Octavian would cautiously sound out Antony's mood and strength before he acted. He fortified his own position before he embarked on the alliance with Antony. Once installed in office, Octavian first brought about the legalisation of his adoption by a law of the people. As Caesar's legitimate heir he could claim all the property left to him, and more important he could place himself at the head of Caesar's considerable band of dependants and followers, or *clientelae*, without which following no Roman politician could hope to maintain any influence. Next, Octavian set up a special court to bring Caesar's murderers to trial. The fact that they were absent from Rome and not able to speak for themselves did not deter him, indeed it facilitated the proceedings, which were initiated and concluded in a single day. All the so-called Liberators were found guilty. They were outlawed and their property was confiscated. Octavian's revenge was not confined to the actual murderers. He condemned several men who knew about the conspiracy but had not revealed it; they were treated as assassins even though they had had nothing to do with the actual killing.

The first stage on the road that led to Philippi had been laid. Other stages were being laid in the east. Brutus and Cassius had refused the tasks asigned to them and gone on to carve out provincial commands for themselves, collecting troops on the way. Cicero had persuaded the Senate to make them the legally appointed governors of the territories that they had seized. This meant that they could legitimately command the troops that they had gathered, but now that they had been outlawed by Octavian they were converted overnight into armed opponents of the state, thus providing Octavian with the excuse to make war on them. This he fully intended to do but he was not strong enough on his own account to carry out his plans. For full scale warfare in the east he needed Antony and Lepidus, and the 22 legions they had gathered in the west. It was necessary, therefore, to revoke the laws declaring them enemies, and then to reinstate them as military commanders in the eyes of the law. This task of undoing the laws making them *hostes* was left to the consul Pedius while Octavian marched north once again to meet Antony, this time on more friendly terms, with Lepidus as ballast.

On an island in a river, probably near to Bononia (Bologna) the three generals met, conferring for two days to thrash out the details of one of the most infamous alliances the world has ever seen. Modern scholars label it the second Triumvirate. Technically there had never been a first Triumvirate; that is a convenient title invented by modern historians to describe the unofficial pact between Pompey, Crassus and Caesar in 60/59. The common denominator is of course that three men met to organise the world to their own advantage, which they could afford to do by dint of their combined military power, political influence, and staggering wealth. The major difference was that the so-called first Triumvirate was a loose and informal private arrangement, whereas the second Triumvirate was a political agreement, legally sanctioned, and properly documented, signed and sealed. The official Latin terminology was *Tresviri rei publicae constituendae*, literally 'three men appointed to reconstitute the Republic'. The necessary law to bring the organisation into being was passed by the tribune P. Titius on 27 November 43.

The Triumvirs were to have powers equal to the consuls, so that they could co-exist with the two supreme magistrates without being overshadowed by them. It was a fiction, of course, since in reality the Triumvirs were much more than the equals of the consuls, and in any case there was scarcely any danger of conflict between the elected consuls and the Triumvirs, because all holders of the consulship in the immediate future would be Caesarian or Triumviral sympathisers. The Triumvirs were empowered to make laws, to nominate magistrates and provincial governors, and above all to assume provincial comands themselves. Pompey and Caesar had shown that the way to gain and hold power was to maintain an influence or even a personal presence in Rome while at the same time commanding troops in one or more of the provinces. On the other hand Caesar's Dictatorship for life had revealed that it was unwise to rob people of the hope of freedom in the future, so the Triumvirs put a five-year limit on their powers, giving the impression that they had merely adopted stringent emergency measures to restore law and order, and once that had been achieved, they would step down.

They did not do so, of course, and after the five years had elapsed the Triumvirate was renewed for a second term. The exact inaugural and terminal dates for the second term are not known, and were perhaps never meant to be precisely outlined, since ambiguity can be very useful to men in power, who wish to keep it without being too blatant about it. Much ink has been used by historians and classical scholars in trying to establish these dates, but they are of legal and academic interest rather than factual importance. From 27 November 43, all power was in the hands of the Triumvirs. After a short time Lepidus was quickly neutralised, and so the two main contenders were Antony and Octavian. Eventually these two men between them dominated the Roman world, and it was of little importance whether or not their powers had officially come to and end. Only a very brave or suicidally inclined person would contemplate bringing a charge of illegality against men who could call on about 180,000 armed assistants.

Their provincial commands were very important to the Triumvirs. Antony was the senior partner, and he knew it. Moreover the others knew it, and acquiesced in his demands for the provinces of Cisalpine and Transalpine Gaul. From this power base Italy could be watched and controlled. Lepidus was confirmed as governor of Narbonese Gaul and all Spain; Octavian was to govern Sardinia, Sicily and Africa. These three areas were not at peace and in some cases not even accessible, but if he could subdue them Octavian would then be able to control the corn supply of Rome. The major thorn in his flesh would be the extensive and experienced fleet of Sextus Pompey, with which he would have to deal before he could hope to control his provinces. All the Triumvirs would govern their provinces via legates, while they attended to business elsewhere, not least a full-scale war against the Liberators.

Marriage ties were proposed to bind the three men together. Lepidus' son was already betrothed to Antony's daughter, as part of the arrangements whereby Antony obtained the post of Pontifex Maximus for Lepidus after the Ides of March. Antony had no other daughters of his own to offer, so it was suggested that Octavian should marry Clodia, the daughter of Fulvia and her husband Clodius. Probably the marriage ties meant very little to each of the participants, but it was a public demonstration of unity for the edification of the rest of the Roman world. The pivotal factor was Antony, who bound each of the other Triumvirs to him personally by the offers of marriage with members of his family. It illustrated his supremacy at the head of the triangle.

The main business of the Triumvirate concerned vengeance for the death of Caesar, by the eradication of the Liberators. Not only the assassins of Caesar, but also their entire circles of supporters and clients were targeted. This ultimate aim necessitated thorough and ruthless preparation. There would be a war in the east with Brutus and Cassius and their followers, but there was much to do in Rome before the Triumvirs could embark on a campaign. They could not hope to achieve anything at all without the support and unquestioning loyalty of their troops, so the generation of that loyalty became the foremost concern of each of the Triumvirs. Their joint armies were in need of rewards and revitalisation; there were veterans to discharge and settle on the land, and new recruits to be found to make up numbers. Eighteen Italian cities were earmarked as the areas where veterans would be given lands. It would not be a very easy or peaceful operation, since it involved the eviction of existing landowners and tenants, but the Triumvirs would deal with that problem when the time came. Recruitment was largely dependent upon ready cash and promises of glory, so that would have to wait for a while. The soldiers were informed of the measures concerning them and the main features of the triple alliance between the Caesarian leaders. Octavian as consul read out to them what had been agreed.

He did not read out to them any details concerning the planned second stage of the programme, namely the infamous proscriptions of many of the most eminent men in Rome. A preliminary list of 17 names was drawn up and sent to the consul Pedius in Rome, where organised mayhem resulted in the removal of these men. The city was closed off and guarded in order to prevent the escape of the intended victims. Pedius may have thought that the horrors were all over, after this grisly episode was concluded, but it was merely the beginning. Many more names were subsequently added to the lists of the proscribed, when the Triumvirs arrived in Rome. It has been suggested that the prime motive for the proscriptions was the appropriation of wealth, since the proscribed men forfeited all their property even if they escaped with their lives. Without doubt, the Triumvirs needed a great deal of money, for all sorts of purposes, and they were not particularly squeamish about how or where they obtained it, but as far as the proscriptions were concerned the acquisition of property and money was a fortuitous by-product. The deaths or expulsion from Italy of enemies, real or potential, was the prime concern. No faction was to be allowed to gain control of Rome and Italy while the war was in progress in the east. Antony could not know how long it would take to bring Brutus and Cassius to battle, nor how long the campaign might be protracted. Caesar had defeated Pompey in the east, but that did not end the war. He had fought in Egypt, Africa and Spain before most of the followers of Pompey had been defeated. Sextus Pompey was still at large, with a powerful fleet which he could use to assist the Liberators. He could blockade Italian ports, disrupting transport and food supplies for the Triumvirs, while at the same time he could carry supplies and troops for Brutus and Cassius. If necessary he could transport their entire armies, so it might happen that even if the first battles were victories for the Triumvirs, the Liberators could regroup and take the war into another theatre altogether. There were endless possibilities, all of which would prolong the war. If the Triumvirs were absent from Rome for any length of time, there would be an opportunity for their enemies to regain power, and then there would be more battles for the control of the city and provinces. The proscriptions were a foolproof insurance policy for the future survival of the Triumvirs.

Rome had seen wholesale murder and rapine before, but that does not excuse the proscriptions of 43. The episode is a stain on all the Triumvirs, equalling anything that Sulla or Marius had done in the civil strife of the recent past. There were some cold-blooded actions, by which the Triumvirs perhaps hoped to demonstrate their ruthless impartiality. They included in the lists of the proscribed certain members of their own families. Lepidus was not averse to naming his brother Aemilius Paullus, who had helped to have him outlawed; Antony put his uncle on the list. The most famous casualty was Cicero. He was included on the initial list of 17 names, along with his brother and nephew. All three met their ends quite quickly, though it is feasible that they could have escaped. They set off to join the Liberators, but vacillated, fatally as it turned out. Cicero's brother and nephew went back to Rome to collect money and property, and were killed. On his way to the coast, Cicero himself was caught by a party of soldiers and died bravely. His head and hands were nailed to the Rostra, after Fulvia had driven pins through his tongue, in revenge for his having spoken the words of the *Philippics* against Antony. The ghastly tales of mutilation may be true, and if so, they do not redound to Antony's credit. It is true that Cicero had ruthlessly put Antony's step-father to death, and that much later he had singled out Antony as an enemy of the state, using his own particular brand of extremely hostile polemic to stir up the Senate and the people against him. Cicero had made all sorts of accusations against Antony that spilled over from political life to deeply personal insults, sometimes so gross that no-one could have believed the accusations to be true. Antony had been seriously provoked, but his treatment of Cicero after his death cannot be defended, even in the context of the barbaric times in which he lived. It is not sufficient excuse to throw all the blame onto Fulvia, since ultimately Antony would have had the final word. If he had not endorsed Fulvia's action she could have made amends. Once his mortal enemy was dead Antony could have allowed him a proper funeral despite his proscribed status, but instead he chose to despatch Cicero to the next world in four separate pieces.

The ancient historians and many modern scholars have sought to exonerate Octavian for his part in the murder of Cicero, usually at the expense of Antony, who takes all the blame without exception. Lepidus escapes blame for the most part, but ought to take his full share. Cicero had voted him a gold statue and tried very hard to win him over to the Senate, but if Lepidus protested about the proscription of Cicero it has escaped the record. It is said that Octavian first tried to save Cicero, but was overwhelmed by his colleagues. The truth is probably very different. While he was in need of support to legalise his position as a commander of troops, Octavian had allied with Cicero to get what he wanted, and Cicero had acquiesced in the alliance because he could not find another army at short notice with which to attack Antony. There had never been any genuine friendship between Cicero and Octavian. When Antony was on the run and retreating into Gaul, Cicero thought that the war was as good as won, and he had made it quite plain at that point in the proceedings that he intended not only to drop Octavian, but to destroy him. Octavian had no reason to like Cicero and would not have derived much assistance from him if he had argued that the orator ought to have been spared. Indeed there was every reason for the removal of Cicero, to prevent him from stirring up further trouble. He had disrupted the peace that Antony had established after the Ides of March, and it was largely due to his efforts that the war of Mutina had even begun. It would have been quite impossible to leave him active and hostile in Rome. It could be said that he had signed his own death warrant with his eloquence. The Triumvirs could not risk the possibility that he might use it to good effect while they were absent. Octavian and Lepidus must bear as much blame as Antony for the death of the orator. It is highly probable that the very first name on the list of 17 proscribed men was Marcus Tullius Cicero, chorused in joyous unison by all three Triumvirs.

When the two-day meeting at Bononia was ended, each of the Triumvirs came into Rome separately, on three different days, each with their entourage and many soldiers, who were lodged in the city, contrary to all custom. There could be no doubt that Rome was now firmly under military rule. Octavian as consul was the first to enter the city. When Antony arrived, Fulvia presumably left the safety of Atticus' house to rejoin her husband. The details of their reunion must remain conjectural. Antony would have much to do, of great import for the history of Rome, but also very significant for his own future. His state of mind can only be imagined. Almost two years had elapsed since the murder of Caesar, when suddenly Antony had been deprived of his friend and patron, and had become sole head of state. From his point of view, he had been dealt with very roughly. He had restored order in March 44 without becoming too dictatorial, he had tried to reconcile opposing parties, and the reward for his pains and what can be described as a certain self-effacement had been distrust, hostility, and ultimately exile. Spared from death by Brutus, he had nonetheless been reduced to the status of a penniless fugitive. It was exactly one year since he had departed for Cisalpine Gaul, not really knowing what his fate would be. During that year he had fought battles against fellow-Romans, suffered defeat, frozen almost to death in the mountains, eaten roots and bark to survive and then staked everything, his reputation and even his life, on walking unprotected into the camp of a former ally. It could not have been the same Antony who now came back to Rome. Some characteristic points of reference were probably still in evidence in his personality, but he could be forgiven if his sense of humour had been somewhat stifled, and his love of wine, women and song had become an empty routine to fill in the few hours he had to spare. The man who had left in 44 was still the old Antony, full of daring, light-hearted optimism and tolerant bonhomie. The man who came back was icily thorough, narrowly focused, and murderous. If the war that he had tried very hard to avoid was now to be fought after all, so be it. But it had to be done properly. There were to be no prisoners. Forgiving was merely a half-measure, and the fate of Caesar demonstrated its ineffectiveness. This time there was to be no mistake. The new lists of names of proscribed men were posted up on 28 November, the day after the act was passed confirming the Triumvirs in power. The killing began immediately, throughout Italy. Pedius died, of stress or a broken heart, or both. Living among carnage, Antony cannot have been other than grim and determined. His thoughts of the future would probably have been confined to the immediate aim of eliminating the enemy. Beyond that he could not make specific plans.

Their chronic lack of money was a serious problem for the Triumvirs, who were forced to resort to extraordinary means to raise cash. Robbing temple treasuries was not so lucrative as it had been, since too many men had already done it, Julius Caesar included. One supposedly sacrosanct source of wealth was the private deposits in the care of the Vestals, hitherto untouched. The Triumvirs appropriated all the savings, no matter to whom they belonged. This act was equivalent to a modern military junta opening and stealing the contents of all the safety deposit boxes in one of the largest banks. The sums raised by various means were not sufficient. The Triumvirs therefore resurrected antiquated taxes which had lain dormant for years, and invented new ones to fill their coffers. The consuls for 42, Lepidus and Plancus, instituted a wealth tax, which even extended to women, hitherto exempt from taxation. The system had a curiously modern flavour — that of self-assessment — which of course led to charges of attempted fraud and ugly accusations. Perhaps the Triumvirs considered that a chronic fear of reprisals would turn everyone into scrupulously honest men, so that self-assessment would yield sufficient funds, without the tedious administration that tax-collection normally requires. But they met unexpected resistance from the women of Rome. Fulvia would not countenance such resistance, but Octavian's sister and Antony's mother joined the ranks of the protestors. Hortensia, the daughter of Cicero's great rival in the law courts, led a deputation to the Triumvirs to point out that women were allowed no voice in the government and ought therefore to remain exempt from taxation. The women declared themselves ready to make any sacrifice if Rome itself should be threatened, but a civil war for which they had not voted was not construed as a threat to Rome. Reluctantly the Triumvirs backed down. The number of women obliged to relinquish a percentage of their wealth to meet the taxes was reduced from 1400 to 400.

Since their avowed purpose was vengeance for Caesar's death, the Triumvirs had a vested interest in elevating him to the highest level, for many reasons, one of which was to ensure that the cause for which they fought was a just one. The Romans had always been adept at finding just reasons for their wars, even those which they had begun themselves without much provocation. The Triumvirs brought to completion the original plans for deification of Caesar that had been mooted while he still lived. He was now officially a god and Antony was a priest of his cult. Octavian of course benefited even more, as the son of a god. The date of his first use of the new title *divi filius* is disputed. There is evidence to show that he was using it by 40, but the better context for it is 43-42 when Caesar was formally deified, if not earlier. When he first arrived in Rome in the spring of 44 and was in need of recognition, Octavian may already have adopted the title for its immediate usefulness in self-promotion. At the beginning of 42 he could make much use of the deification to advertise himself as well as his pursuit of vengeance for his adoptive father. He reminded people of the divine Caesar at every opportunity, employing *Divus Julius* as the watchword of the army, and later inscribing sling bullets with the name at the siege of Perusia. Antony too equated himself with divinity when he was hailed as the new Dionysos in the east, and sometimes as Hercules. Caesar himself had claimed descent from Venus. But these associations were mythical and distant, symbolic but unrealistic; Octavian's association was with a living, memorable person, who combined symbol with reality. In that sense he was already assured of rather more credibility than Antony, whose lavish play-acting as the new Dionysos impressed but did not convince the easterners.

On a more practical level, all Caesar's acts as Dictator were confirmed. Each of the remaining senators and magistrates took an oath to observe and maintain them. Antony had attempted to bring this about in 44, but now he made certain of it. It was not simply a demonstration of loyalty to Caesar; it was the foundation for the future. Antony's past achievements and the basis upon which he fought the coming war, indeed his whole destiny, were linked to Caesar, just as much as Octavian's future goals were rooted in Caesar's groundwork. If Antony had chosen to fight on his own account without reference to Caesar, his cause may have been a just one in his own mind but not necessarily in the minds of the Roman people. Thus it was as a lieutenant of a dead commander that he fought the Liberators, no matter that he was a consular and a Triumvir in his own right. Octavian's career as Caesar's successor was already mapping itself out, but Antony had still to create an Empire for himself.

The Roman world was about to witness another civil war, which threatened to split it right down the middle. Polarisation into separate halves was almost complete, Caesarians in the west and the Liberators in the east. In Rome and the west, Antony and his colleagues reassigned the magistracies and provincial commands to fill the gaps as the original postholders fled to Sextus Pompey, or to the Liberators, or were killed. The consulship was obviously the most important magistracy, and must be secured for the next few years. The consuls for 42, Lepidus and Plancus, had already entered office. For 41, P. Servilius Isauricus and Lucius Antonius were designated, and for 40, Asinius Pollio and Gnaeus Domitius Calvinus. These were preponderantly Antonius' men, inherited from Caesar. For the consulship of 39, when presumably the wars would be concluded, Antony and Octavian designated themselves. As for the other magistracies, the Triumvirs were accused of handing out commands as rewards for their friends, but whilst there may have been a grain of truth in this it is highly improbable that unsuitable or dubious characters would have been placed in important positions, however much the Triumvirs may have owed these people some sort of favour. When they left Rome, Antony and Octavian required firm control of the western provinces via their chosen men, whom they could trust. The entire western world was thoroughly Caesarian and it was intended that it should remain so for some time to come.

The east was almost exclusively in the hands of the Liberators. Brutus and Cassius had seized territories for themselves, raising troops by whatever means were available to them. Brutus recruited troops in Macedonia, where he captured Antony's brother Gaius, sent out as governor of the province. Cicero advised him to kill Gaius. For a while the noble Brutus refused, but

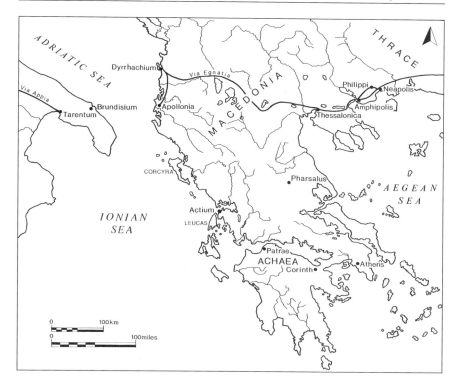

9.   *Map of Macedonia and Greece where Antony fought several battles. He was with Caesar at Dyrrhachium and Pharsalus; he fought and defeated Brutus and Cassius at Philippi, and he met disaster at Actium.*

Drawn by Graeme Stobbs

finally gave in, probably after he had heard of the death of Cicero, when he sent orders that Gaius Antonius should be executed. Antony therefore began the war against the Liberators with more than one death to avenge. The capture and then the death of Gaius reduced the Caesarian foothold in the east to nil. Dolabella ultimately fared no better. He started well but finished badly. As his consulship ended he went to take up his governorship of Syria, travelling via Macedonia and Thrace. He defeated and killed Trebonius, the Senate's legally appointed proconsular governor of Asia.

The contest for Syria began. Cassius travelled by sea and arrived first. He was already a respected figure in the east, having fought with Crassus in the disastrous Parthian campaign, and he had rendered good service in Syria in the aftermath of the retreat. With a secure following and established in a secure base, he was able to divert and retain the four legions sent by Cleopatra from

10.   *Gold Aureus of 42 with the head of Brutus on the obverse and military trophies on the reverse. The victories being celebrated are those of Brutus' troop-raising activities in the east. Casca Longus, named on the reverse, was one of Brutus' legates.*

© *British Museum*

Egypt to aid Dolabella. These four legions, added to the eight he had already raised, brought his force to a total of 12 legions, all loyal to his cause. When he and Brutus joined forces, the Liberators were supreme. Dolabella was blockaded in Laodicea, where he could hope for no rescue or means of escape. In despair he committed suicide. The Liberators now had most of the eastern provinces under their sway, and control of the sea as well. They possessed ships of their own and had a potential ally in Sextus Pompey, who was spiritually associated with the Liberators by dint of his long-standing quarrel with the Caesarians. Fortunately for the Triumvirs, neither Sextus nor the Liberators actively pursued the possibilities that this alliance held for them, preferring to act independently. The perceived threat to the Triumvirs remained just as strong, despite the lack of unity among their enemeis. They could not know that Sextus and the Liberators would remain aloof from each other. As far as the Triumvirs were concerned, they would either have to fight both parties separately, or worse, they might suddenly find themselves opposed by a formidable naval and military combination.

Men, money, and ships were assembled to begin the wars against both the Liberators and Sextus Pompey. Lepidus was to remain in Rome with some troops to enable him to keep order. He surrendered seven legions to Antony and Octavian to help them with the campaign. As a preliminary move, Octavian sent his friend Salvidienus Rufus to Sicily in an attempt to wrest the island from Sextus Pompey, and to clear the Mediterranean of his fleet. Much depended on the success of this venture. The transport of troops from Italy to Greece to begin the campaign would be far less hazardous if Pompey's ships were removed from the scene, and if he had been forced to relinquish Sicily, the Triumvirs would immediately gain control of the lucrative corn supply, and also a naval base. Unfortunately the attempt was a disaster. Sextus Pompey's sailors were much more experienced than those of Salvidienus, and easily drove him off. The Triumvirs did not waste any more time on this particular project, opting instead to combine forces and concentrate on the campaign in the east. War was largely a seasonal occupation, and crossing the Mediterranean was inadvisable except in summer, so any delay would cost more in supplies and soldiers' pay, and lessen the chances of being able to start the campaign that year, while at the same time the Liberators would gather strength, more supplies and more money, and perhaps even bring in the Parthians on their side, which was a very dangerous prospect. It was not a hysterical alarm without foundation. Brutus did in fact send Quintus Labienus, the son of Caesar's bitter personal enemy Titus Labienus, to Orodes of Parthia to ask for help, but this news only emerged later, after the Caesarian victory at Philippi. Quintus Labienus stayed in Parthia when he heard that Brutus and Cassius were vanquished.

At the outset of the war, Antony had only a few ships, and could not carry the whole army across the sea in one magnificent invasion. He took advantage of the news that Queen Cleopatra had despatched an Egyptian fleet to aid him and Octavian. Her allegiance was to the memory of Caesar, the father of her son Caesarion, so she readily aided the chief lieutenant and the heir of Caesar. Her expensive gesture came to nothing in the end, since the fleet was caught in one of the sudden Mediterranean storms and was wrecked, but the reported progress of her ships troubled the Liberators sufficiently to send out their own fleet under the command of Staius Murcus and Domitius Ahenobarbus, to search for them and to destroy them, or at least to prevent them from reaching Antony. In this brief respite, with the enemy fleet drawn off from Brundisium, Antony rapidly ferried eight legions across the Adriatic under Decidius Saxa and Norbanus Flaccus, who landed on the unguarded coast of Macedonia, then moved rapidly eastwards along the Via Egnatia to Thessalonika, and from there to Thrace to guard the passes controlling the route from Asia to Europe. Thus, by his quick action, Antony managed to gain a foothold in the east. His vanguard presumably did not launch itself into the unknown; it is probable that Antony had received some intelligence of the enemy's movements on land as well as in the Mediterranean, and had acted as rapidly as he could to take advantage of it, before Murcus and Ahenobarbus blockaded the port and before Brutus and Cassius could assemble an attacking force. The speed of the operation took Brutus and Cassius by surprise, and forced them to move to meet the threat. They brought their armies into Thrace and moved westwards along the Via Egnatia to block Norbanus and Saxa, who withdrew to Amphipolis and dug in. With sure connections to their coastal supply base at Neapolis, Brutus and Cassius camped to the west of a place called Philippi. The scene was set for the decisive battle.

In order to ferry the rest of the army across the Adriatic, Antony required favourable westerly winds, over which he had no control, and more ships to combat the blockading forces under Staius Murcus and Domitius Aenobarbus. He was hampered by his lack of oared ships, but even so he sometimes succeeded in extricating his cumbersome sailing transports, keeping the enemy fleet at a safe distance by artillery fire from engines mounted on barges. But it was a slow business, not much improved until he finally obtained oared ships from Octavian, when the attempt to win Sicily was abandoned, and the two of them allied to bring their combined forces against the Liberators. For a brief moment Staius Murcus drew off from Brundisium, and once again Antony seized his chance. He and Octavian ferried the bulk of the army to Dyrrachium. Next Antony had to find the armies of Brutus and Cassius, and bring them to battle as rapidly as possible. Delays would only increase his difficulties over supplies for men and horses. It was like Pharsalus all over again, but that meant that Antony would have no illusions about what he was up against, and could draw on considerable experience to guide him when the time came.

Octavian was too ill to march after he had reached Dyrrachium, so Antony started out eastwards along the Via Egnatia without him. He had no doubt heard that Norbanus and Saxa were entrenched in Amphipolis, and by now he would know where Brutus and Cassius were camped. Antony marched rapidly to join his eight legions in Amphipolis, where he left only one legion in garrison, and took the rest of the army towards Philippi. He sent out a small party to reconnoitre the strength of the Liberators' camp. Brutus and Cassius had utilised every advantage of the ground. They had camped across the road, Brutus in the northern camp with mountains to protect his flank, and Cassius

11.   (*Opposite*) *Plans of the two battles of Philippi showing the various stages of the main episodes*

(a)   *Philippi First Battle October 42*
      Antony builds a causeway across the marsh to cut the communications of Brutus and Cassius, and get behind Cassius' camp.

(b)   *Antony defeats Cassius and drives him from his camp. Cassius withdraws to the north east, and later commits suicide. At the same time Brutus defeats Octavian and captures his camp, but Octavian survives by hiding in the marsh.*

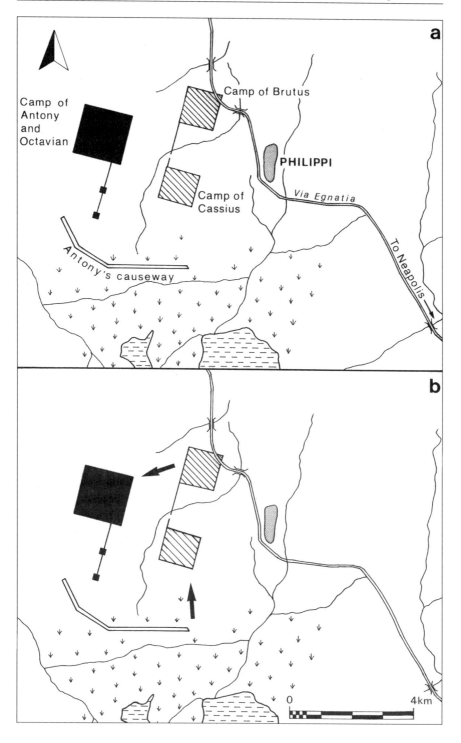

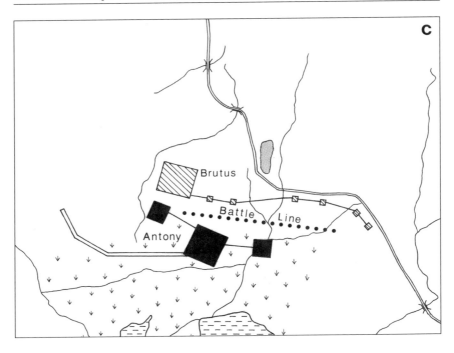

11 (c) Philippi Second Battle November 42
Brutus moves into Cassius' camp, and Antony continues his outflanking
movement. Brutus builds small posts to keep pace with him, but offers battle in
mid-November. Antony and Octavian eventually encircle him and drive him off.

Drawn by Graeme Stobbs

in the southern camp with his flank protected by a marsh. They had also
entrenched themselves behind well-guarded earthworks. Antony kept up an
outward display of confidence that he perhaps did not feel, made camp, and
decided that the Liberators must be cut off from their supplies, and the only
way to do that was to make a causeway across the marsh and try to come round
to the rear of Cassius' camp. He began the work in secret and was not
discovered for some time. By now Octavian had joined him, travelling in a
litter from Dyrrachium, still very ill, but determined to play his part in
avenging Caesar, and more than likely very anxious not to allow all the credit
for any victory go to Antony alone. He could possibly have dealt with a
defeated Antony limping back to Dyrrachium, or even with the news that
Antony had been annihilated and was dead. In either case, Octavian would
take some of the blame for the disaster, then he would regroup and launch

another campaign, in a desperate last bid for vengeance. But, if Octavian did nothing except lie in bed at Dyrrachium while a victorious Antony won the war, he would be obliterated for ever. Antony would be the sole avenger of Caesar, sole champion of the soldiers, sole political conqueror. Octavian had to be there, wherever the battle was to be fought.

As a distraction to divert enemy attention from the causeway that he was building across the marsh, Antony drew up his forces to offer battle each day, but eventually Cassius realised what was happening to threaten his rear, and began to build counter works. It was here that the first battle of Philippi began, in a skirmish over the defences. Antony passed a few cohorts across the causeway, and Cassius attacked them, so Antony committed more troops to rescue them. Brutus' men could see the fighting to the south and began an attack of their own, imagining, possibly, that they would be able to finish Antony by a swift flank attack . In the confusion, Antony took Cassius' camp, but Brutus took Octavian's, as though the two armies had swivelled round clockwise to end up at a 90 degree angle to their original positions. Neither side could hold onto what they had gained, and had to return to their bases. Octavian had prudently hidden in a bog, so he fortunately evaded capture. Later he said that he had been warned in a dream not to stand in the battle line, which may even have been true: stranger things have happened. The most important result of the first battle was that Cassius, driven from his camp, gave up much too soon, thinking erroneously that Brutus had been defeated and killed. Instead of waiting for properly authenticated news he assumed the worst and committed suicide.

Brutus was now alone, but still in a fairly strong position. He entrenched, and began the waiting game, knowing that the supply problem would weaken Antony if only he could hold out for long enough. There was no need to offer battle in these circumstances, but it is probable that Brutus' officers and even some of the soldiers thought that Antony would be quickly defeated. Their blood was up, and they wanted action. They may have worn Brutus down, demanding battle. At any rate, for some inexplicable reason, about two weeks after the first battle, Brutus drew up his army in battle order. Antony probably could not believe his eyes. He accepted the challenge straight away. This time Octavian's men held firm, though they were pushed back. Antony tried to outflank Brutus, which may have been a feint, because when Brutus plugged the gap by sending out his reserve, Antony switched to an attack on the centre. As Alan Roberts points out in his book on Antony, it may be that Brutus simply fell into an elaborately prepared trap devised by Antony, or perhaps Antony watched carefully, seizing the chance once he recognised where the weakest spot was, and then throwing in everything he could spare to exploit it. Either scenario reflects great credit on him for ingenuity and promptness of execution.

Brutus escaped with four legions, and Antony pursued him. One of Brutus' officers, Lucilius, delayed the pursuers by impersonating Brutus and allowing himself to be captured. He demanded to be taken to Antony, who of course knew immediately that he had been duped. He did not display any anger, excusing the soldiers who had made the mistake by saying that he was rather glad that it was not Brutus, because he would not have known what to do with him. He and Brutus had been acquaintances, if not friends, and had been drawn together in the political arena. Antony probably was genuinely glad not to have to give the order to execute him. There was no deeply personal animosity between them, unlike the rancour between Antony and Cicero, even though Brutus had been directly responsible for the death of Gaius Antonius. In the end Brutus helpfully committed suicide, and his followers either fled in different directions, to Sextus Pompey or to Ahenobarbus, or they came over to Antony and Octavian. One of the most famous converts was the poet Quintus Horatius Flaccus, who remained in Octavian's circle until his death, and is known to us as Horace. The rest were killed, and it is said that Octavian delighted in cruelty, exacting the last ounce of vengeance from the deaths of some of the conspirators. He made a father and son throw dice to decide who should be spared, and laughed as the one chosen to survive committed suicide over the body of the other. The legend states that the soldiers hailed Antony as the victor, but reviled Octavian; the tale is usually connected to those of Octavian's cruelty but, if there is any truth in the revulsion felt by the troops, it probably stemmed from the fact that Antony had done all the hard work while Octavian was ill. Perhaps Antony himself did not stop to reflect that courage takes many forms, one of which is the ability to overcome illness and take at least some part in the fighting. There is no need to doubt that Octavian was genuinely ill, but from Antony's point of view, the activity of the past months had probably been comparable to wearing a ball and chain. Antony could have managed quite well if he had possessed only Octavian's troops and not Octavian himself, for it is likely that he thought of Caesar's heir as more of a liability than a supportive colleague.

After the victory, Brutus' body was brought to Antony's camp. He covered the corpse with his own cloak and ordered an honorable funeral for him. Octavian demanded that Brutus' head should be cut off and thrown down at the foot of Caesar's statue in Rome. In view of his treatment of Cicero, Antony was hardly in a position to refuse on ethical grounds, so Octavian had his wish. At the same time, Antony exacted revenge on Hortensius, the officer who had killed Gaius Antonius. Appropriately, Antony had him put to death near Gaius' tomb.

There may have been an overriding sense of anti-climax. The Liberators were dead or dispersed. The battlefields were to be cleared up. There were hundreds of troops to be reorganised, paid off and settled on the land. The provinces were to be reassigned, the whole of the east required delicate restructuring, the government of Rome and Italy was to be set on a firm foundation, friends were to be sifted from enemies, financial affairs were in chaos, the food supply was threatened, Sextus Pompey was still at large. The list was endless. Most important, the Triumvirs, now for all practical purposes whittled down to two, not three, men, had to protect and prolong their powers. They could not disband their armies entirely, and therefore had to find a legitimate excuse for keeping them. From the combined troops of their own armies and those of the Liberators, the Triumvirs formed 11 legions, five of them for Octavian and six for Antony, but since they were already in the east, where Antony would need troops, Octavian was to lend two of them to Antony. When he returned to Italy, Octavian was to reclaim two legions for his own forces from the legions stationed in the western provinces. Octavian's task was to settle the veterans on lands in Italy and to pursue the war against Sextus Pompey. His provinces were to be Spain, Sardinia, Corsica, Sicily if he could win it from Sextus, and Africa. If Lepidus was to be trusted, he was to be assigned to Africa in Octavian's place, but if it proved to be true that he had been making overtures to Sextus and might have allied with him, then he would be deleted from the Triumvirate, and Octavian would keep Africa. It sounds like a plot to discredit Lepidus, but on this occasion it did not pay off. Lepidus remained part of the Triumvirate for a few years longer, though not as a decisive element in the wars or decision making.

Antony took the lion's share, reflecting the seniority of his position. He was to govern the two Gauls, through his legates Calenus, Plancus and Ventidius, with about 17 legions. Cisalpine Gaul would be governed by Pollio, pending its integration with Italy, which was to be common ground for both Antony and Octavian. With a preponderant influence in the west, unassailable at the head of large armies, Antony himself would remain in the east, taking up in due course the great Caesarian project of war against Parthia. Lepidus hardly seemed to count any more. Having arranged the entire Roman world according to their own wishes and for their mutual benefit, the two Triumvirs went their separate ways. Octavian returned to Italy, where his main task would be to settle the veterans on lands promised to them at the meeting at Bononia, at the beginning of the Triumvirate. Antony remained in the east, which was in chaos after the upheavals caused by Brutus and Cassius. Some states had sympathised with the Liberators, some had resisted, others had tried to remain neutral but had been forced to contribute money or supplies. The result was the same whichever side they had chosen. Many of them were impoverished or damaged in some way, and it could not be assumed that every city or state would welcome Mark Antony with open arms. There was much to do, and Antony travelled far and wide, repairing damage, hearing cases, exacting tribute, meting out punishments where necessary. The chronology is difficult to re-establish, since most sources merely tell us that Antony went to Athens for the winter, as though that was all he did, oblivious to all else. Common sense dictates that he could not simply leave the huge army that was reassembled after Philippi, nor could he ignore the immediate needs of the eastern Roman provinces and the free states. Stability in the east was the prime necessity, which entailed placing the troops at strategic locations under reliable commanders, and tactful handling of both Roman governors and client kings. That was not something that he could achieve in a few months.

When all was reasonably quiet, Antony did go to Athens, the city of his student days. He could not know it yet, but he was about to embark on the final, most glorious decade of his life.

5   Eastern promise

Antony enjoyed himself in Athens in the winter of 42-41. He seemed to regard his stay there as a holiday — which, after all, he deserved. The years since the death of Caesar had been strenuous and nerve wracking, so after he had toured the eastern provinces and safely quartered the troops, Antony cast off his role as soldier and became a leisured tourist. Generous and open-handed, he also became a benefactor of Athens. He liked to be seen at the theatre and the games, dressed in the Greek style. He went to lectures, and joined in debates. His voluntary return to Athens suggests that as a student he had appreciated all that the city had to offer, and appreciated it now for different reasons. It had the advantage of being not too far from Rome but conveniently placed so that he could keep in touch with the eastern territories. Athens satisfied several criteria at once. Communications were as easy as it was possible to be in the ancient world, the climate was mild enough in the winter, the pleasures were numerous, and Antony was no doubt glad to indulge himself in culture and learning as an escape from the carnage of the past few years.

The Greek way of life appealed to him, because it liberated him from the strict but frenetic atmosphere of Rome, where even as Triumvir and conquering hero he would have to be watchful at all times for anything his enemies might use to bring about his downfall. In Athens he could be himself in a way that he could never be in Rome. Since he was in a position of unassailable power, he could afford to indulge himself, and no-one minded that he kept the company of actors and actresses, or that he enjoyed food and wine, late hours and leisure.

When spring came he had to attend to business once again. The Roman provinces of the east comprised Asia and Bithynia (occupying western and northern Turkey), and Syria. Their larger neighbouring territories were ruled by kings supposedly favourable to Rome, and there was a host of lesser kingdoms and territories under a variety of rulers. All these lands required much fine-tuning, especially if Antony was to persuade them to disgorge the funds he needed to finance his various ventures and pay the troops. Reparations had to be made to those states which had suffered at the hands of

12.   *Mark Antony appears on the obverse of the gold aureus of 42, styled as IIIVIR,
or Triumvir. On the reverse the god Mars is depicted with his foot on a shield and
a spear in his right hand. Lucius Mussidius Longus, named on the reverse, was
one of the four officials (*Quattuoviri*) who for a short time from 42 to 40 issued
gold coinage with portraits of the Triumvirs. The use of personal portraiture on
Roman coins was a relatively new departure, first utilised by Caesar.*

© *British Museum*

Brutus and Cassius, and those that had sided with the Liberators would have
to be handled delicately. He left Lucius Censorinus with six legions to look
after the Greek states, and took two legions with him to Ephesus. There he
was hailed as the new Dionysos, an appropriate divinity for Antony, the god of
wine and beneficence. To a stern Roman, full of *dignitas* and *gravitas*, this was
highly suspect, but it was the eastern custom, so Antony played the game
according to the eastern rules. Pompey had received the same treatment when
his eastern conquests had brought him fame. His earthly divinity lent Antony
power in the east, and to protest that he was a mere mortal would only
undermine it. Besides, his new-found status as a living god provided a
counterweight to Octavian's claim to be the son of a god.

Antony based himself at Pergamum, and summoned representatives from
the eastern states to meet him there. His first demand for ten years' taxes
payable in one year was greeted with disbelief. Brutus and Cassius had made
similar demands to finance their war and consequently had stripped most of
the east already. Now the victor wanted even more. One of the spokesmen
pointed out that, since Antony was powerful enough to ask for a second levy
of taxes after the Liberators had already levied the first one, then perhaps he
would be good enough to arrange for a second summer and a second harvest.

Antony liked frankness, especially when it was combined with wit, so he arrived at a partial compromise, settling for nine years' taxes payable in two years. Having secured his cash and supplies, Antony could be magnanimous. Several cities which had supported Brutus and Cassius were pardoned. They had for the most part been coerced and in any case it was preferable to forget the past and make a new start. There was more to be gained from a slightly damaged but extant economy than an annihilated one, however much the desire for revenge might have dominated Antony's thoughts. He tried to make amends for the more serious depredations of the Liberators, and readjusted some boundaries here and there. Athens and Rhodes were given or restored to the overlordship of some neighbouring islands, not solely for the political power that this would bring them but for economic reasons.

Cassius had taken some Jewish prisoners on his tour of the east, and now Hyrcanus of Judaea arrived at Antony's headquarters to ask for their release, which Antony readily granted. He also heard another deputation from Judaea making accusations against Herod, son of Antipater, but when Antony met Herod personally in Bithynia, he found in his favour. The sources do not preserve much of the detail of Antony's administrative arrangements in the eastern territories. Consequently, from the few facts that are known, it seems that Antony merely reacted to requests rather than taking the initiative himself. He has therefore been accused of dilatoriness in sorting out the complicated affairs of the east, as though he had no real political interests and was merely determined to take advantage of anything that might be beneficial to him, allowing the rest to follow its own course. On the other hand if he had gone about his tasks in typically Roman fashion, coldly logical and brutally efficient, he would have earned a reputation for arbitrary arrogance and high-handedness.

That was not the way to deal with the east. It was probably simple enough to survey the scene from afar with an unemotional attitude, to analyse the problems and then to suggest what had to be done, where boundaries should lie and who should be subordinate to whom. But to apply such neat schemes would have been disastrous. The eastern cities had a long history and a complex and intricately entwined structure. Their relationships were volatile and changeable, so it was easy to upset the delicate balance of power but difficult to repair the damage once that had been done. Much later, the ever-cautious and consummate statesman Augustus dealt very tactfully with the east, playing a patient, low-key waiting game, interfering only when it was absolutely necessary. Antony probably reasoned that there was no need to redefine the eastern territories, uprooting the ruling houses which had lent aid to the Liberators. He dealt with each case on its own merits, provided always that his interests and those of Rome were not compromised. It may seem that he put his own interests first but, though he arrogated power to himself, it was not necessarily selfish or megalomaniac tendencies that motivated him. Personal power brought with it the capacity for patronage, which in turn increased personal power, which would be very beneficial to him in Rome. That was also what the east generally understood. The concept of the strong, semi-divine leader and protector took precedence over any sense of corporate identity. A treaty made with Rome was perfectly understandable in a context where some of the city states had a longer history than Rome herself, but in the east the personal representative of Rome was always regarded as the more important factor, no doubt because it was more practical to contact an individual whose habits and characteristics were known, rather than an anonymous and possibly arbitrary body such as the Senate. Pompey had made sound administrative arrangements for the east for which he made every effort to obtain ratification from the Senate, but nonetheless he did not relinquish his position as influential personal liaison between the various eastern cities and Rome, nor did he give up the potential source of wealth that this position automatically conferred on him. Antony simply followed suit, especially since his financial needs outweighed any other consideration, and probably always would. Apart from his own personal needs, he had a large army to pay and feed, and an equally large administrative personnel to organise.

The states bordering on the Parthian Empire required subtle wooing. Even when there were no hostilities with Parthia, the Romans needed to maintain good relations with these border states in order to keep open the major routes through them, and to obtain reliable intelligence about Parthian intentions. In wartime, the border territories would be in the front line if the Parthians attacked, and consequently in a good position to cut off any Roman forces which might invade Parthia. It was prudent to be on good terms with rulers of those territories through which one needed to march home, either confidently as victors or more especially in abject retreat. The loyalty of the border cities and states had to be earned or bought, and then assiduously cultivated.

The territory of Galatia in modern central Turkey was ruled by Deiotarus, who had sided with Brutus and Cassius during the civil wars. Antony did not supplant him. It was better to rely on a king who knew his people and terrain than to try to find a suitable substitute who might change allegiance or be ejected as soon as the Romans were removed to a safe distance. In eastern Turkey the kingdom of Cappadocia was in turmoil because there were two rival claimants, Archelaus (also called Sisina) and Ariarathes, both of whom were fighting for the throne. Antony made a tour of inspection and installed Ariarathes as king. It is said that he had a brief affair with Glaphyra, the mother of Archelaus, but in this instance he may not have initiated the proceedings himself. The episode sounds much more like an effort on Glaphyra's part to influence Antony, and a shameless exploitation on Antony's part of whatever came his way. It also demonstrates that he made decisions quite independently of attempts to seduce him. His choice of Ariarathes may have suited the needs of the moment, but he had to revise his opinion later. Ariarathes did not prove loyal, and in the end Glaphyra's son Archelaus was given the kingdom of Cappadocia.

Between them, Deiotarus of Galatia and Ariarathes of Cappadocia watched large areas of the east in close proximity to Parthia. There remained Armenia, the continual source of tension in Roman and Parthian politics, but before attempting to solve that particular problem, Antony turned his attentions to Egypt. He needed vast quantities of money and also a fleet, and though he had set about obtaining the former and building the latter, the resources of Egypt would further his projects considerably. He did not want to go to Egypt personally, because that would place him in the position of suppliant, and make it seem as though he was subordinate to Queen Cleopatra. Playing the part of victorious Roman Triumvir, he sent his envoy Quintus Dellius to Alexandria. Somehow, Dellius persuaded Cleopatra to come to Tarsus to meet Antony, ostensibly to answer charges that she had aided and abetted Cassius. The charge was monstrously false, since she had despatched the Roman legions of Egypt to help the Caesarian general, Dolabella. It was quite beyond her control that these legions had found themselves opposed by many more legions, and had made the sensible choice to join Cassius, instead of fighting what would most probably have been their last battle. Cleopatra had also sent her fleet to help Octavian and Antony, and had been thwarted by the storms which wrecked it. Perhaps the charge that she had helped the murderers of Caesar was made to ensure that she rose to the bait, but in that case, all that she needed to do was send a haughty reply. If Antony wanted something from her, let him come to Egypt. Since she went instead to Tarsus, sailing up the river Cydnus on her famous Royal barge, it must be supposed that she wanted something from Antony. Her ambitions were later portrayed by Octavian as nothing short of world domination, but she probably never aimed so high. A secure throne in a secure territory were her foremost concerns, and after that a secure future for her son Caesarion. She was already educating the child as her successor, and the fact that he was also Caesar's son represented no small threat to Octavian.

Cleopatra may have possessed a lust for power, but it was probably limited to Egypt and whatever lucrative territorial additions she could attach to it, primarily for the revenues they would bring with them. While in Rome as the guest of Caesar, she would have met Antony, perhaps on several occasions, and she would have made an estimate of him and his main attributes, his strengths and weaknesses, talents and deficiencies, and most of all his usefulness. She probably liked him, even though she may have intended to use him when she came to Tarsus. Common-sense dictated that it was wise to be on good terms with the Roman Triumvir who commanded armies throughout the east. She may have wished to sound him out before he set foot in Egypt, leaving herself with the option of keeping him at arm's length. After all, the Romans had such a happy knack of ultimately annexing territories that they first entered casually, converting them into provinces before the inhabitants had a chance to think twice. By going to Antony before he came to her, she perhaps hoped to avoid this fate.

The meeting has been portrayed in countless different ways. Shakespeare has probably never been bettered, even though film producers have lavished great care and enormous sums on recreating the scene. The truth was probably more fantastic than the fictional scenarios. Cleopatra was determined to make a stupendous impression, and she did possess the wealth and the means to do so. She was clever, shrewd and determined, seductive rather than physically beautiful. It is said that her most seductive attributes were her mellifluous voice and her conversation, and there is no reason to doubt the legend. She was a linguist of some distinction, having learned among other languages the native Egyptian tongue, the first of the Greek Ptolemies to make the effort to speak to their subjects in their own language. There may have been more than the social motive behind the learning of languages, of course, because those who do not speak a language sufficiently well must rely upon interpreters, and can be so much more easily cheated or betrayed. Cleopatra did not intend to be cheated or betrayed, in either the political or economic sphere. She had a good head for business and finance, and a decided sense of her own and her country's importance.

According to Appian, Antony fell for her on the spot, ready to obey her slightest whim, gradually becoming quite oblivious to Rome and all it stood for. This is part of the Augustan repertoire, where Antony is depicted as weak, spineless, bewitched by the evil Queen. It is a clever portrayal because it condemns Antony and provides the excuse for reviling him, but at the same time it excuses him because it presupposes that he was in the grip of a power that was stronger than him, more evil and infinitely more to be feared. Cleopatra was both a foreigner and a woman, one who did not know her place, and therefore an enemy on two counts. By placing on her all the blame for the civil war between Antony and Octavian, the Romans avoided the slur on their own history. They converted Octavian into a saviour and Antony from a Roman general into a pathetic victim, and then they wreaked revenge on the Queen who had caused his downfall. Octavian built up Cleopatra into the arch-enemy of Rome and then defeated her, so he made the Romans grateful for what he had achieved, so grateful that they did not seem to mind that one of the direct results of his achievement was that he took over the whole of Egypt, together with its vastly wealthy Treasury, and kept it as his personal preserve.

Later authors have modified or embellished the legend of Antony and

Cleopatra. Romantics cling to the love story. Cynics opt for the theory of bald political expediency and nothing more. Moderates try to blend the two extremes. The bare facts are that Antony dined with Cleopatra on her fantastic ship on the river Cydnus at Tarsus, and that after the meeting he went to Alexandria and spent the winter of 41-40 exclusively in her company. Later she bore him twins, a boy and a girl, whom he acknowledged as his own. There is so much room for multiple reinterpretations of these few pieces of solid information that the only recourse is to choose what to believe and then to make the facts fit the theory. Political considerations most certainly did play a large part in what happened. If, for instance, it had been Antony who went back to Italy and Octavian who had elected to remain in the east, sooner or later he and Cleopatra would have come face to face over some issue or other. Speculation as to what then might have been the fate of the world would occupy a separate chapter. Octavian was much younger, much more calculating and much colder than Antony; perhaps it is even true to say that he was more narrowly focused and at the same time more flexible about the means that he used to achieve his ends. He would have used Cleopatra in a different way and, though he was not averse to sexual affairs, he would probably have kept her firmly in her place as Queen of Egypt. The wealth of the country would have bound him to her, and he would have taken it all in the end, but the final act would probably have constituted merely a footnote in history, and literature, plays and films would have been the poorer for it.

After the famous visit to Tarsus, Cleopatra returned to Egypt, and Antony promised to follow her to Alexandria as soon as he had attended to the administration and settlement of the provinces. There was some trouble in Syria, where the populace was restive because of the heavy tribute imposed by Rome, and there was no lack of aspiring leaders, some of them backed by Parthia, who knew how to exploit the unrest. Antony's response was to launch a raid on Palmyra, poised between the two great Empires of Rome and Parthia but free from direct Roman or Parthian control. He wished to make a demonstration of his potential power, but the reasons for his actions are obscure, perhaps even deliberately deleted from the record to make him seem irresponsible. There was little to show from the raid, because the Palmyrenes simply decamped and abandoned their city, taking their belongings with them across the Euphrates and waiting until Antony's soldiers went away. Appian accuses Antony of creating a terrible mess in Syria by this unprovoked attack, and then imposing further tribute. Before he had sorted out the problems, so the story goes, he went off to Egypt because he was so besotted with the Queen. The accusations are unlikely to be true, but lack of evidence in Antony's favour makes it impossible to refute them entirely. Antony had first hand knowledge of Syria, its problems, and its advantages, and he also knew that it was feasible to invade Egypt from Syria because he had been there, done it, and survived. He would not turn his back on Syria until he had settled affairs there. He placed Decidius Saxa in command, one of the generals who had led his advance guard into Macedonia before the battle of Philippi, and as trustworthy as any of Antony's lieutenants, if not the best. With Saxa in charge and the province settled, Antony went to Egypt.

The Alexandrians liked Antony and his sense of fun. They said that in Rome he wore his tragic mask, but for them he exchanged it for his comic mask. He formed a club called 'The Inimitable Livers' dedicated to pleasures of all kinds. Various anecdotes about his behaviour have passed into legend, but are perhaps not too far from the truth, and reveal something of the man and his relationship with Cleopatra. On a fishing trip where he caught nothing, he sent his slaves underwater to attach some newly-dead fish to his line, and then he hauled them in, pretending to have caught them all at once. The next day Cleopatra sent some of her own slaves underwater to attach a salted fish to his line. He landed it, his ruse of the previous day exposed, but taking it in good part, and no doubt quite certain who the culprit was. Such fun and games, if not true in their specific details, are probably representative of Antony's Alexandrian adventures. It may have been politically expedient for the foremost Roman general in the east to woo the Queen of Egypt to ensure her allegiance to Rome, and it may have been shrewd manoeuvring on Cleopatra's part to entertain the Roman Triumvir to keep her country intact, but their relationship certainly went beyond that.

Antony's plans for the east and what he intended to do with the rest of his life are not known for certain. It is assumed by some scholars that Cleopatra drove everything out of his head so that he had no concerted plans at all. Others maintain that he had a strategic outline that is now lost. With or without a considered policy in mind, it is assumed by both his supporters and his detractors that he must have planned the attack on Parthia immediately after Philippi, because that is what he eventually carried out. Caesar had planned to do it, and Antony was in most respects Caesar's heir in this matter, and there would be eternal glory in carrying Roman arms into the Parthian Empire to avenge the defeat of Crassus. The project was probably always in his mind, but he did not move immediately after Philippi. An expedition of such enormous importance could not be begun lightly on a moment's notice, and the east must be secured before an army could be despatched beyond the territories under Roman control. But it was only after the near outbreak of civil war between Antony and Octavian, averted by the pact of Brundisium, that Antony began to move against Parthia, and when he did it was in response to an attack on Syria, which at first he sent his general Ventidius Bassus to repel. Until then his interests in the west were as strong as his claims on the east, and he may have decided to put his Parthian expedition on hold, loitering with intent in Egypt while awaiting the outcome of events in Italy.

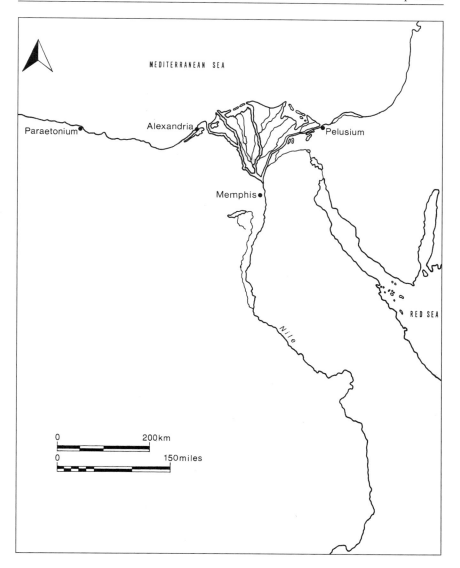

13.   Map of Egypt.

   Drawn by Graeme Stobbs

14.   *Head of Cleopatra from North Africa, now in the Museum at Cherchel, Algeria. This head has also been identified as Cleopatra Selene, the daughter of Antony and Cleopatra who married king Juba of Mauretania, during the early Empire.*

Courtesy Agence Nationale d'Archéologie et de Protection des Sites et Monuments Historiques, Algiers

While Antony enjoyed the company of Cleopatra in Alexandria, Octavian was faced with very difficult problems. His main concerns after Philippi were centred on Italy and the settlement of the time-expired veterans. This was a thankless task because it involved the eviction of existing farmers and an enormous redistribution of lands. Octavian no doubt anticipated trouble but perhaps had not foreseen the tremendous complications that arose. He smoothed the path at first by tact and diplomacy, but then met with active opposition, aroused and fostered by the consul Lucius Antonius and his sister-in-law Fulvia. The other consul was Servilius Isauricus but, as Dio says, the real consuls were Lucius and Fulvia. The whole episode is strange and probably distorted. Lucius had two potential levers to use against Octavian. First he espoused the cause of the soldiers of Antony's legions, implying that Octavian had not treated them fairly. Octavian cooperated by allowing Antonian representatives to supervise the settlement of Antonian veterans, which removed the difficulty. Thwarted of serious trouble-making in that direction, Lucius changed tactics and began to stir up the displaced farmers, which was already an emotive topic and needed no encouragement. Whichever way Octavian turned he was certain to be wrong-footed. It seemed that Lucius and Fulvia were determined to bring him down.

The soldiers could see clearly that war was looming, and since they would be directly involved in any fighting they tried to avert it by arranging a conference between Lucius and Octavian at Teanum. The two men met as planned and discussed the problems, but without result. Things went from bad to worse. Lucius and Fulvia fled to Praeneste, making great play of their fear of Octavian. When people declare their fear of someone or something it usually means that they will make belligerent efforts to protect themselves, and in turn the object of their fear has no choice except to do the same. Octavian recruited troops from any and every source, putting his friend Marcus Vipsanius Agrippa in command of them. He recalled his legate Salvidienus Rufus who was marching to Spain with six legions to take over as governor there. While Octavian was engaged in this desperate recruitment drive, Lucius marched on Rome, where he made politically correct noises about dismantling the Triumvirate and restoring the Republic. He was given a legitimate command by the Senate and set out to meet Octavian's troops, but Agrippa moved quickly around him and managed to cut him off from Rome. Panicking, Lucius marched north to Perusia, where Octavian lost no time in besieging him. It was a short-lived affair, which ended in February 40 with the town's destruction by fire, perhaps the result of an unfortunate accident. Octavian put to death anyone who had had the remotest connection with the death of Caesar. Lucius was allowed to go free, since he was Antony's brother and it would cause tremendous problems to kill him. He was sent to Spain, ostensibly as governor, but in reality a sort of prisoner, closely watched by Octavian's men.

95

Antony's part in all this is shrouded in mystery. No-one knows for certain whether Lucius and Fulvia had taken it upon themselves to foster Antony's interests without his knowledge, or whether they acted on his instructions. When Lucius talked of restoring the Republic, presumably Antony was to feature as the senior statesman in this new scheme of things, no longer the anomalous Triumvir but as traditional and lawful consul. Blood ties do not guarantee loyalty, but it is difficult to believe that Lucius was about to undermine his brother and instal himself as supreme magistrate. It is even more difficult to believe that it was part of Fulvia's plans to supplant her husband and deprive him of political power. The question is, how much did Antony know of the escalating war? Plutarch exonerates him by insisting that the first news of what was happening came to Antony while he was in Alexandria. Dio, on the other hand, is certain that Antony had engineered the whole incident, but sat on the fence while it was played out, pretending that he did not know about it. Between these two extremes there are several possible permutations of the facts, without a hope of resolution.

It stretches credulity somewhat to suggest that Antony knew nothing of what was going on in Italy. Despite the difficulties of travelling in winter, friends who wanted to help him and enemies who wanted to discredit him would fall over themselves to inform him. It is feasible that he was so absorbed with Cleopatra that he refused to be bothered with news from Rome, only springing into action when it became clear to him that things were going badly there. During the build up to the war he gave no clear instructions to his generals in Gaul, who did nothing decisive to help Lucius, but that does not necessarily prove Antony's innocence. The case for the defence has to prove that he genuinely knew nothing of the activities of his wife and brother, in which circumstance he was a victim of misplaced zeal exercised unwisely on his behalf. The case for the prosecution has to find evidence that Antony realised what was happening but made no effort to stop it, perhaps hoping to utilise the situation to his own advantage, but meanwhile to wait until he was recalled to Rome to sort out the problem. The worst scenario is that Antony dreamed up the whole scheme in order to create such upheaval that not only would Octavian be discredited, but that Antony would be the one man who could restore order, with consequent sole power and access to all the armed forces of the Roman world, which he could then dispose of as he wished. It had been done before, and Antony had witnessed it, and learned from it. Appian was clearly aware of these implications. Through the mouth of Antony's henchman Manius, Appian puts forward one possible interpretation. Manius reminded Fulvia that, as long as there was peace in Italy, Antony would stay with Cleopatra, but if there was war he would have to return, or would even be recalled by the Senate, to take charge of the situation.

Events did not unfold in that way in the end. Antony left Egypt for Athens with problems erupting all around him. Perhaps in response to his demonstration of strength on their borders with Palmyra, the Parthians overran Syria early in 40, undoing all that Antony had achieved there. His governor Decidius Saxa was killed. Herod fled from Judaea to Rome and a Parthian sympathiser, Antigonus, was installed as ruler in his place in Jerusalem. Though the greater part of the east was in ferment, Antony could do little to restore the balance, unless he was prepared to ignore events in the west and perhaps suffer a total eclipse there. Octavian had emerged from the Perusine war more successful and stronger than ever. The Antonians were in retreat. Civil war seemed inevitable.

Most of Antony's associates and his immediate family had fled after Perusia fell. Ventidius Bassus rounded up the Antonian troops and remained in Italy. Antony would eventually send him the east to re-establish the situation there while he attended in person to the degenerating relationship with Octavian. Fulvia and the Antonian general Plancus travelled to Greece. Since his legions had gone over to Octavian, Plancus had little choice. Fulvia was not likely to find sympathy in Rome, so she hastened to her husband. Her role is not clear. She may have acted independently in what she saw as her husband's best interests, or she may have been his willing agent, acting under his orders. It seems that Antony was not grateful. There may have been an irrevocable split between them on account of the highly emotional issue of Cleopatra. Even if Antony had been totally innocent of any relationship with the Queen, Fulvia would probably have been consumed by justifiable jealousy that her husband chose to spend so much time with another woman. She may have understood that political needs outweighed her personal concerns, but it was evident that Antony had mixed business with pleasure on a grand scale, and his relationship with Cleopatra was not limited to the diplomatic sphere. There may have been furious rows about the matter. At any rate Antony left Fulvia in Greece, though she was very ill. Perhaps he did not know that it was to be a fatal illness. He never saw her again.

He could not afford to waste time in arriving in Italy, but he has been accused of callousness in leaving the woman who had worked energetically on his behalf, and whom he was generally supposed to love very deeply. The legend fostered by his enemies has perhaps distorted both contemporary and historical perception of his actions. In other circumstances he would perhaps have been praised for stoic heroism in leaving the woman he loved for reasons of state, spurning his own emotional needs and fulfilling his duty like a Roman. If he had survived, vigorous and victorious, or if Octavian had died young, our own perception of Mark Antony might have been very different.

Antony's mother Julia also fled from Italy, and found refuge with Sextus Pompey, who at some point made friendly overtures to Antony, suggesting an alliance. The exact chronology is not established, but if Julia was confident of a friendly reception it suggests strongly that negotiations had already begun before Perusia fell. Antony replied to Sextus in favourable terms but did not commit himself entirely. He promised that if he could not come to terms with his rivals he would ally with Sextus, but if he succeeded in making peace with Octavian, then he would endeavour to reconcile Sextus and his followers with the Senate and people of Rome. This reply was no doubt made for public consumption. It was an honourable and reasonable decision, with just enough of a threat of strong action if negotiations with Octavian failed. Control of a fleet in the Mediterranean was an important consideration, one which Antony could not afford to ignore. Instead of entering an alliance with Sextus, he chose the less inflammatory alliance with Domitius Ahenobarbus, who had kept his fleet together after Pharsalus and had been a free agent ever since. Domitius was a Republican and therefore less repugnant to the Senate than Sextus, especially since he had not chosen to harry the coastal ports and disrupt the food supply as Sextus had done. For Antony he was a politically correct associate and a useful assistant in helping to patrol the seaways. Together Antony and Domitius approached Brundisium, only to find that there were large numbers of Octavian's troops there, and the town had closed its gates against them.

Antony almost certainly concluded that Octavian had ordered his troops to guard the town and not to let him land there. Grimly he set about besieging the place, and sent troops to take the nearby town of Sipontum. Octavian's response was to send Agrippa to retake it, and Publius Servilius Rullus to drive Antony off from Brundisium. Antony attacked before Servilius was ready for him, and drove him off instead. He killed many of Servilius' men and many more soldiers prudently changed sides and joined Antony. The soldiers were the saviours of the situation at this point. They had no desire to fight each other, having for the most part known each other when Caesar was in command of them all. Their loyalties were divided now between the two successors of Caesar, and besides they were tired of war, especially the kind of war which brought them no lasting glory, no rich booty from foreign lands and only the prospect of more war until eventually either one man emerged as sole victor or the antagonists came to some agreement.

The outbreak of another civil war was averted by diplomacy and compromise, in September 40. Octavian's equestrian and non-military friend Maecenas became his spokesman, and Pollio was intermediary for Antony. Also present at the initial talks was Lucius Cocceius Nerva, who was not a partisan of either party. By the time that the negotiations began, the balance had tilted in Octavian's favour. He had ended his marriage to Fulvia's daughter, Clodia. She was very young, and the marriage had probably not been consummated. Now he married Scribonia, the sister of Lucius Scribonius Libo, whose daughter was married to Sextus Pompey. Octavian's intention

15.   *A gold aureus dated to 41, issued by Gnaeus Domitius Ahenobarbus. The portrait may be of Ahenobarbus himself, but the attribution is not certain. The temple of Neptune was obviously chosen to mark Ahenobarbus' career, first as a naval officer of Brutus, and then an independent admiral after Philippi. He made an alliance with Antony in 40, adding his naval power to Antony's forces. He remained with him until the last moments at Actium, then deserted to Octavian, but he was very ill by then and died soon afterwards.*

© British Museum

was transparently obvious. He did not marry for reasons of affection, but for political expedience, as a preliminary to a political alliance with Sextus. Antony probably felt himself completely upstaged, and may have regretted not having allied with Sextus early in the year, when he had the chance. Octavian was now in a strong bargaining position, and a fortuitous event made him even stronger. In the summer of 40 Antony's legate in Gaul, Fufius Calenus, suddenly died. Octavian immediately took over Calenus' legions without even the hint of a struggle. He declared that he did so to protect Antony's interests, but of course his own interests were hardly neglected when he took over the troops. It was a tremendous advantage to him to be able to control Gaul and also to be able to call upon so many extra soldiers. His main concern was no doubt to pre-empt the considerable problems that would have arisen if Calenus' legions had fallen into the hands of someone else, especially if that someone were to pick up the threads that Lucius Antonius and Fulvia had dropped when they were defeated at Perusia. The inevitability of it all, and the supremely fortunate timing of events from Octavian's point of view, probably made Antony think that his luck had deserted him. He acquiesced in the loss of his command of Gaul and of his troops, though he received some compensation by way of extra troops for his later eastern campaign.

The agreement reached in the autumn of 40 is known to historians as the Treaty of Brundisium. Its terms redefined the division of the Roman world and determined Antony's future. From now on he would focus exclusively on the east. The division between east and west was tidier than the previous arrangements that had been made after Pharsalus. The new dividing line was placed in Illyria at a hitherto unknown town called Scodra, now in northern Albania. Octavian received all the western provinces. His main tasks were to win back Sicily and Sardinia from Sextus. Lepidus was left in command of Africa, out of harm's way. Antony was to contol all the east, and was to have greater powers to reorganise and restructure it. Then he was to deal with the Parthian problem. For a short while there seemed to be an optimistic accord between the two Triumvirs, celebrated probably throughout the Roman world, but the evidence for the celebrations is limited. All that is left is a trace element of the response to the Treaty of Brundisium. 'Concord' was the catchphrase of the day. Coins were struck with the legend M. ANTON. C. CAESAR IMP. refering to the two men as military commanders, with a representation of the goddess Concordia prominently displayed, so that people were left in no doubt of two things, the definite presence of armed force, but also the restraining influence of harmonious relations. A monument at Casinum in Italy celebrated the same Concord. There were no doubt many more such artistic flourishes, now lost.

Despite the optimistic outlook and celebratory adulation, Antony had lost preeminence in the west and was never to regain it. Italy was initially intended to be common recruiting ground for both Triumvirs, but Antony's influence there also waned for the principle reason that after 39 he was permanently absent and therefore unable to sustain the personal contacts that were necessary for the maintenance of client relationships, and for the nurturing of loyalty among the troops and potential recruits.

Perhaps Antony did not think of this long-term result when he signed the latest pact with Octavian. The two Triumvirs went to Rome in the late autumn, to demonstrate their solidarity and to organise the government to their joint satisfaction. There were gift exchanges, and sacrifices. Octavian gave his elder sister Octavia to Antony in marriage. Both were recently bereaved. Fulvia had died in Greece, and Octavia's husband Marcellus had died, too recently for her to marry according to Roman custom. Formalities such as those never stood in the way of men like Octavian and Antony, but since they had to be seen to do things correctly according to the social rules, they persuaded the Senate to give the necessary permission for Octavia to remarry before the proper mourning period was over.

The sacrifices concerned one of each of Octavian's and Antony's lieutenants. Antony's associate Manius had been one of the prime movers in the lead up to the Perusine war, and according to tradition he was the man who advised Fulvia that, if there were to be a serious war in Italy, then Antony would be recalled and would forget Cleopatra. If he had given this advice, or was deemed to have said something along those lines, then Antony was obliged to demonstrate that he would not tolerate such revolutionary talk which implied that turmoil in Italy was to be stirred up and then used for personal reasons. It was of no consequence whether Manius had never breathed a word, or whether he had expressed an opinion of his own, or whether he had acted under the orders of Antony himself. There could be no hint that Antony had perhaps had a personal interest in discrediting Octavian and installing himself as head of the government. What counted was the elimination of suspicion, so that Antony emerged whiter than white. Manius had to go.

More puzzling is the removal of Salvidienus Rufus, who was one of Octavian's closest and long-standing friends. They had been together in Macedonia just before Caesar was murdered, and they had sailed back to Italy together, along with Marcus Vipsanius Agrippa. Antony declared that, while he was preparing for the siege of Brundisium, Salvidienus had sent word to him that he was prepared to desert Octavian and join him. The tale may be as simple as that. Perhaps Salvidienus had grown tired of Octavian's single minded pursuit of supremacy, which entailed the subordination of all his friends to that one purpose. Agrippa was content to be the second man in Rome after Octavian, and never wavered from this loyal self-effacement. Salvidienus may have wanted more, and possibly thought he could obtain it from Antony. There are many more sinister permutations of the facts, but there is no available information to support any specific theory. Octavian was careful to dispose of Salvidienus by fully documented legal means. The Senate obligingly passed the last decree (*senatus consultum ultimum*). Salvidienus was recalled from Gaul and condemned to death.

The air was now cleared. All the machinery was in place for the Triumvirs to take charge, but the path to power was never smooth. Sextus Pompey had obtained very little from his efforts to negotiate with either of the Triumvirs, who were plainly more concerned with their own immediate needs than they were with his. His immediate response to his lack of positive gain was to attack the coastal towns of Italy yet again and to disrupt the food supply of Rome to such a degree that famine became a real threat. His strategy worked. The people of Rome rioted. They pelted their erstwhile hero Octavian with stones when he attempted to speak to the mob. Octavian had to be rescued by Antony's troops. The situation could not be tolerated, but neither Octavian nor Antony were prepared to go to war against such an experienced adversary as Sextus. They possessed neither the ships nor the sailors to go to war at sea, and they had not developed the naval expertise to use them even if they could have produced them at short notice. Fortunately Octavian was still married to

Scribonia, and was therefore one of Sextus' relations by marriage. Antony suggested that the relationship should be made to work for them, and that Octavian's brother-in-law Scribonius Libo should be asked to act as intermediary with Sextus. In negotiation, the Triumvirs had to concede that Sextus would retain control of Sicily, Sardinia, and Corsica. They were primarily interested in restoring the food supply of Rome so that the rioting would cease and so that their own credibility would be revived. They could do nothing to wrest from Sextus his absolute command of the islands and the predominance it afforded him over the coastal areas of the whole Mediterranean. They undermined his support by offering his soldiers the same rewards as their own, but that was a hollow victory, and not even an immediate one. All else would come in good time. Sextus perhaps understood all this when he entertained the two Triumvirs on board his flagship, after they had signed the Treaty of Misenum in summer 39. His admiral Menas suggested to him that he could solve his problems all at once if he simply cut the cables and sailed off with his guests, tipping them overboard somewhere in the open sea. Sextus nobly refused. He would have gained little, and would have merely ostracised himself more than ever. Rome would not automatically accept him because he had disposed of the Triumvirs. He took a chance with the Treaty of Misenum, which restored the status quo and did him no harm. He was made an augur, and promised the consulship for 33. He was also promised control of the Peloponnese for five years, which was to be handed over to him from the eastern territories under Antony's control. If it had actually come about, it would have meant that Sextus had a foot in both camps, and a presence in each of the Triumvirs' territories.

Peace was restored among the Romans for the time being. Octavian had emerged in a much stronger position now that he controlled the western provinces, but there was much to do in Italy. Security still depended on the goodwill of Sextus. Octavian's ability and political shrewdness were not in doubt, but Antony was his equal in political matters and his superior in the military sphere. There was perhaps no need for Antony to worry about the loss of the western provinces, and the encroachments made by Octavian. After all the youth was frail, always ailing, and perhaps might even die, then Antony could come back to Rome to take charge, preferably after a victorious campaign against the Parthians. A victory would bring him considerable kudos and enhance his standing in Rome. It would enable him to reorganise the east and stabilise it, making it secure for the future, with each provincial governor and each carefully chosen client ruler owing his or her supremacy to Mark Antony. Such a vast range of wealthy clients in his entourage could do him nothing but good. The avenger of Crassus would enjoy considerable prestige even among those Romans who were not his clients. He would be a potent force, and equal to anything that Octavian could achieve.

16.   *Silver coin depicting Antony and his wife Octavia. The legend on the obverse, partly worn away in this example, reads M. ANTONIUS. IMP. COS DESIG. ITER. ET. TERT. referring to his military command as Imperator, and the fact that he was consul designate for 38. The reverse shows Bacchus flanked by two intertwined serpents.*

© *British Museum*

Antony is so inextricably associated with the east, and his reputation for having 'gone native' is so indelible that it is tempting to assume that in the autumn of 39 when he set out for Athens with his new wife Octavia, Antony had turned his back on Rome totally and irrevocably. He never returned to Rome, but that was perhaps more a result of circumstance than intention. At the end of 39 he was looking towards Parthia, and he was all-powerful in the east, but he was still a Roman official, brought up with a Roman philosophy, and with a Roman perspective on the world. He was a soldier with Roman ambitions of conquest, but that did not mean that once he had conquered he would forget Rome. His command was sanctioned by the Senate and he had taken the precaution of having all his acts, past and future, ratified before he left the city. Knowing full well by dint of bitter experience how the political climate of Rome could be manipulated, he made every effort to strengthen and legalise his position before he embarked on a distant campaign. He thought ahead to the time when he would return to Rome, and would embark on the next stage of his career.

He spent the winter of 39 in Athens with his new wife, and prepared for the coming campaign. He did not travel far and wide, but he was not idle during the sojourn in Greece. He dressed as a Greek civilian, freely enjoying the

Greek way of life, but his leisurely appearance did not preclude activity. The ancient sources depict the tremendous contrast between his household in winter, peaceful, unhurried, and uncluttered, and the sudden burst of energy in spring, when his house became a military headquarters in all its noisy splendour, with couriers coming and going, queues of officers at the door, and Antony himself dashing about clad in Roman military dress. Appearances can be deceptive, and in this instance have been used to imply that Antony did nothing for a few months and then burst into ill-planned action at the last minute. But he could scarcely have forgotten the east for a single instant while he was in Athens. During his stay in Egypt, the Parthians had attacked and begun to take over vast areas including Judaea, Syria, and Asia Minor. The instigator of these attacks on Roman and independent eastern territories was Quintus Labienus, the son of Titus, who had been sent by Brutus and Cassius on a mission to the Parthian court and had consequently found himself isolated after the battle of Philippi. Having nowhere to go, he threw in his lot with the Parthians and worked in conjunction with Pacorus to overrun the eastern cities and place them under Parthian control. Labienus advertised his exploits by means of his coinage, displaying his portrait and his newly adopted titles celebrating his military successes. He called himself Imperator, and also 'Parthicus', which to a Roman would normally have meant that he had conquered Parthia, but to Labienus, the title signified his change of allegiance from Rome to the camp of Rome's traditional enemy.

Antony had attended to the situation in the east as soon as he was able. During the summer of 39, while he negotiated with Octavian, he sent Ventidius Bassus to restore order in Syria and Asia Minor. This able lieutenant concentrated all his energies on the renegade Labienus, who was soon driven into unseemly flight. He was last heard of in Cilicia, and then disappeared. Next Ventidius drove the Parthians out of Syria. There will have been a great deal still to do after the fighting was over, but Ventidius' arrangements for consolidation are not recorded in detail. He would need to distribute his troops for the winter to guard routes and strategic points, especially those on the frontiers with Parthia, and most important of all he would need regular and dependable food supplies. He levied tribute from various cities, especially those which had either assisted Labienus and the Parthian Pacorus, or at least not put up a very determined resistance to them.

All through the winter of 39 and during the early part of 38, Ventidius will have been in communication with Antony, keeping him informed of events. Once he had reached Athens, Antony could communicate with Ventidius much more easily and much more rapidly than he was able to do while he was in Rome. In Greece Antony will have been able to make a better assessment of what was needed in the east, and he would be better able to direct events from a distance. Indeed in Athens he was in the best position to keep in touch

17.   *Silver denarius of 40, showing the head of Quintus Labienus, the son of Titus Labienus, who had been sent on a mission to Parthia by Brutus, to try to organise an alliance with the Parthian king Orodes. Meanwhile Antony and Octavian won the battle of Philippi, so Labienus remained where he was, and was instrumental in instigating the Parthian invasion of Syria. His title Parthicus would normally signify that he had conquered Parthia, but he adopted it to proclaim his alliance with king Orodes. Ventidius Bassus' campaigns drove the Parthians out and put an end to Labienus' activities.*

© *British Museum*

with both the east and the west. If he expected further trouble from the eastern cities and the Parthians, he would certainly have expected trouble from the west as well. He would need to know what Octavian was doing. After the loss of his Gallic legions and his western provinces to Octavian it is extremely unlikely that Antony trusted his Triumviral colleague in the slightest degree.

For this reason, his house in Athens will have witnessed many a coming and going from both halves of the Roman world, but while his despatches to and from the east were official, as part of his eastern command sanctioned by the Senate, his agents in the west would need to be more circumspect. Octavian would definitely be watching him as closely as he watched Octavian, so the leisured life in Athens, in conjugal bliss with Octavian's sister, may have been a deliberate screen to declare to the Roman world in general and to Octavian in particular that their political relationship was progressing smoothly. If such it was, his plan backfired on him, because Octavian was able to use it to disseminate a portrait of Antony as an ineffective and even disreputable general and politician. There are few contemporary literary sources that can be said to depict Antony in his true colours, since many have been lost and what survives is a thoroughly reworked record, moulded to suit Octavian's purpose. Occasionally a fortuitous discovery of an inscription or a fragment of one can serve to set part of the record straight. The famous series of inscriptions from the city of Aphrodisias have been dated to the Triumviral period and throw some light on the state of affairs pertaining in the east. One of the inscriptions refers to a man called Stephanos, who was authorised to act in Antony's name in the east, but the text of the inscription reveals that Octavian also sent instructions to Stephanos directly, without going through Antony's offices first. There is insufficient evidence on which to base any firm or wide ranging conclusion, but it would seem that there was a potential source of conflict in this system, since it implies that Antony's command of the east was not quite as exclusive as he had been given to understand. It is not known if Antony enjoyed the same rights in the west that Octavian seemed to be able to exercise in the east. To be sure, Antony would have some say in what happened to his clients in the Italian cities, but the case just outlined in the east is not comparable. Octavian's monarchical tendencies revealed themselves long before he restored the Republic and became Augustus.

In spring 38, Antony began to move. There was much preparatory work to do. The eastern cities and states required more adjustment and fine tuning, which could be done successfully only on a basis of sound local knowledge and careful balancing of immediate needs against long term plans. Two things happened which delayed Antony, almost a repeat performance of the events of 40 and 39. The Parthians launched another attack on Syria, and at the same time Octavian summoned Antony to the west, where the situation in Italy was deteriorating rapidly. Ventidius was once again put in charge of operations against the Parthians and Antony sailed to Italy. Octavian was in deep trouble. The peace treaty with Sextus Pompey had lasted barely a year. Very shortly after it been concluded, Octavian divorced his wife Scribonia, on the very day that she gave birth to his only child, his daughter Julia. Sextus Pompey took the hint that their relationship was ended, and recommenced his raids on the Italian ports and harbours, disrupting the food supply all over again. In consequence Octavian was in very bad odour in Rome, though his situation improved somewhat when Sextus' admiral Menodorus deserted to him, bringing men, money and ships, and relinquishing control of Sardinia and Corsica to him. From then on Sextus Pompey and Octavian were at war. Sextus was the better admiral and strategist, and easily defeated Octavian in two separate encounters. Antony wasted valuable time and expense in coming to Brundisium to meet Octavian, only to find that Octavian was not there. The young man may have been ill. He was always ill at crucial moments, though that did not usually prevent him from being at the right place at the right time. This time, however, he did not keep his appointment. Antony went off in a justifiable rage and made his sentiments known in an open letter to

Octavian. He then dashed to Syria, arriving in midsummer. Ventidius had succeeded in stabilising the situation once again, so all was not lost. He had brought Pacorus to battle in north-eastern Syria, at Gindarus, and there he had defeated him utterly. The Parthian leader's head was brought to Ventidius as a trophy, and he sent it on a tour of the eastern cities as proof that he had defeated the enemy decisively.

The problems of Judaea were almost resolved, too. Herod had been recognised as king of the Idumaeans and Samarians, but not yet king of Judaea, because Jerusalem was still in the hands of the Parthian favourite Antigonus. As soon as he was able to spare the troops, Ventidius sent a contingent to assist Herod, while he himself marched to Samosata on the right bank of the Euphrates, where Antiochus, king of Commagene, was sheltering Parthian refugees. Ventidius besieged the place. It was quite outside Roman control, so Ventidius' siege was designed to be construed as an aggressive punitive act to restore Roman supremacy. Antony arrived at Samosata in late summer and took over from Ventidius, who went back to Rome to hold a well-deserved triumph in November 38. The Triumvirs allowed their legates to celebrate this supreme honour, but later on when Octavian had gathered all power to himself, the triumphal procession through the streets of Rome became a rarity, a jealously guarded reward, restricted to members of the Imperial family. Yet it was Octavian who fostered the rumour that Antony was jealous of his legate's successes, and that the death of Ventidius some short time later was not altogether a natural occurrence. There was another rumour that Ventidius had accepted bribes from Antiochus, and had delayed the siege of Samosata on purpose, so that he ruined Antony's chances of taking the city. In consequence, it is said that Antony cashiered his former friend, and sent him home in disgrace. This is nonsense, of course. It is a contradiction in terms for a disgraced general to celebrate a triumph. The fact that Ventidius retired after he had reached this apogee perhaps gave rise to the theory that he had been cashiered. Tremendously successful, but unemployed, Ventidius would be an object of curiosity in Rome: if he was half as good as people said he was, then why did he not go back to the east where he belonged, at Antony's side? Retirement in the modern sense was not a concept that the Romans understood, but Ventidius was not a young man, and he had had a harsh early life. He was probably tired, perhaps not very healthy. As for the possibility that Ventidius' death was suspicious, Antony had much to gain with Ventidius alive and well and working for him in Rome, whereas he could not possibly hope to achieve anything by killing him. If he had been jealous, he would certainly not have allowed his friend and reliable general to hold a triumph in the first place; he could have made any one of several excuses to keep him out of the public eye. If he had been really incensed, he did not need to wait until after Ventidius' triumph to dispose of him. It would have been quicker, more economical, and far more credible to arrange a little accident in Syria. Nonetheless, Antony may have had an ulterior motive of a far different kind in sending Ventidius home to make a great display in the city. Octavian had enjoyed very little success in the battles against the renegade Roman Sextus Pompey, but Antony's lieutenant had twice prevailed against that most dangerous of enemies, the Parthians. The celebrations proclaimed Antony as much as Ventidius, and plunged Octavian into the background. It was a war of words and attitudes, posturing and upstaging.

After the departure of Ventidius, the siege of Samosata slipped into impasse quite quickly. Antony negotiated a settlement and returned to Athens for the winter of 38-37. There was nothing more to be done in the east until the next campaigning season started in the spring of 37, though the day-to-day administration of the Roman provinces and the careful watch on the client states continued without a break. Antony's administrative work is unrecorded, but as supreme Roman commander of the whole of the east, his delegated officials and the client kings would ultimately report to him. This routine labour would be taken as read in the ancient world, so perhaps nobody bothered to record it for posterity. There were after all greater things at stake during these years, and since it was Octavian who finally emerged perhaps not unscathed but definitely supreme, it is his exploits that fall into the limelight.

The west had not escaped turmoil in 38. Agrippa had won notable victories in Gaul, where there had been serious problems in Aquitania. Octavian had battled on against Sextus Pompey but had gained nothing. In fact his record was abysmal. Tactfully, Agrippa refused a triumph for his Gallic campaigns, because the contrast between his successes and Octavian's failures would have been too great. As the year was drawing to a close, Antony received a visit from Octavian's friend Maecenas, who had come to ask for assistance against Sextus Pompey. Since it would have been unwise to march into Parthia with such a potential flashpoint behind him, Antony agreed to meet Octavian once again to come to some arrangement. Either Sextus must be defeated decisively, or integrated fully into the Triumviral government. The latter was a remote possibility, because neither Antony nor Octavian wanted Sextus as an ally in the Mediterranean, and they certainly did not want him in Rome because he could stir up far too much trouble for them there, even though they held the whole Roman world in thrall by military dictatorship. The only choices that Antony could make were to assist Octavian and hope that this time he would defeat Sextus, or to take on the war himself. He got together a fleet of 300 ships, and sailed to Brundisium in spring 37.

For the third time, he found himself in difficulties when he arrived. Brundisium was closed to him, and the town authorities would not allow the fleet to sail into the harbour. There is some disagreement in the sources about this event, where perhaps the previous debacles have been confused with this

18.   *Head of Mark Antony, with double chin and worry lines between his eyebrows. The rugged face is of an older and more experienced general.*

Courtesy Musée Archéologique, Narbonne. Photo Jean Lepage © Musées de Narbonne

one. At any rate, for some reason Antony sailed on to Tarentum, and that was where Octavian came to meet him. It is said that Octavia, Antony's wife and Octavian's sister, played an important part in reconciling the two men. Perhaps the story is true, especially if Antony had been refused admittance into Brundisium for the third time in succession. His temper would hardly have been amiable, nor would Octavian have been in a good mood, because he was forced to ask Antony for help in a war that he had been trying to win for some time.

The agreement made at Tarentum in 37 embraced more than just the immediate needs of the two Triumvirs. Octavian was to receive 120 ships from Antony, to replace those that had been destoyed by Sextus, or wrecked in storms. These Antony parted with straight away. The deal was supposed to benefit Antony too. In his Parthian campaign he would have more need for soldiers than ships and sailors, so Octavian agreed to give him 20,000 men. One may be permitted to wonder if Antony really believed that he would ever receive them, or if Octavian ever intended to do more than sign the document that promised the men to Antony. He never relinquished them all. What Antony finally received was a pathetic contribution, when it was too late.

After the exchange of ships and men had been agreed, the Triumvirs turned to their joint needs. Technically, they held no legal power because the Triumvirate had been set up for a fixed term of five years in 43, which meant that at the end of 38 it had run its term. For the time being, of course, it was highly unlikely that either of them would be challenged, and no-one had yet begun to shout the name of Lepidus as a candidate for sole government. Antony and Octavian were still in power because they held most of the armed forces of the Roman world, and besides they were the two men most able to put an end to the depredations of Sextus Pompey and thus restore freedom of the seas and the food supply of Rome. The Roman mob for the most part had enough sense not to bite the hands that fed them, and the Senate was muzzled after the savage proscriptions of 43. But there remained the problem of political correctness. Neither Antony nor Octavian could hope to continue on this nebulous basis for too long. At the present time of emergencies and disasters, there was not much danger of legal wrangling, but a close examination of the Triumvirate would reveal so many loopholes that the Triumvirs would not risk having their powers placed under scrutiny. Questions as to whether there was a fixed legal term or whether the Triumvirate was open ended until the Triumvirs resigned were probably being asked in many a private household, but no-one had asked them in the Senate, and probably never would. But it was a risk that could not be allowed. Being in a hurry, Antony and Octavian did not bother with too many time consuming formalities. They renewed their powers for another five years, and shortly afterwards the position was legalised by a law of the people of Rome.

Theoretically the new terminal date was to be the end of 33, but in 38 probably neither of the Triumvirs lost any sleep over that particular dilemma. Their present predicament absorbed their whole attention. Octavian and Agrippa had to build up a new fleet and train their crews, and Antony had to reorganise and stabilise the east. Neither task was a sinecure.

6 Parthia

The negotiations at Tarentum were prolonged until the late summer or early autumn, which meant that the prospect of campaigning in the east during that year was now very remote. The campaign was therefore relegated to 36. During the intervening months, there would be plenty of time for Antony to make an assessment of where he stood. Octavian had gone from strength to strength, and had declared for all to see the direction that he was following. His marriage to Livia Drusilla in January 38 was an important political step, no matter how much he may have been bowled over by her charms and however much he may have loved her. He had married her in an impatient hurry, manipulating the laws in order to do so. He allowed no difficulties to stand in his way, even though Livia had to be divorced from her first husband Tiberius Claudius Nero, by whom she already had one son, and was pregnant for the second time. Since the paternity of the second child was not in doubt, and there was no hint of previous relations with Octavian, Livia was duly divorced and remarried according to Octavian's wishes. Her two children by her previous marriage were the future Emperor Tiberius and his ill-fated younger brother Drusus, who died in Germany in 9BC after a fall from his horse. Octavian had a daughter by Scribonia, and no doubt he hoped for more children by his new wife, to ensure that he would have male heirs and could pass on whatever he possessed to reliable successors of his own blood. It was not to be, but his marriage brought him other benefits. Livia Drusilla was the daughter of Marcus Livius Drusus Claudianus. Her background was impeccable and she was well connected with the most noble families of Rome. She would play an important role in bringing over to Octavian powerful allies from the senatorial body, men whose sense of their own dignity might have been affronted by an alliance with an Octavius, but not by an alliance with a scion of the Claudian house.

There was still the problem of Sextus Pompey for Octavian to overcome, and there was every possibility that he would find the task too difficult, but whatever the outcome of that particular struggle, by now Antony would be aware that Italy and the west were closed to him unless he asserted himself.

Despite his marriage to Octavia, Antony was not exactly a close associate and trusted friend of Octavian, and would have to work very hard to remain one step ahead. It did not matter that Antony's agents were working for him in Rome, nor that he himself could perhaps look forward to future consulships and high offices. His absence from Italy had gradually given the advantage to Octavian, who was continually in the public eye, and continually exploited to the utmost every political expedient that he could muster to advertise himself, putting himself into the best possible light. He did not do so in a vacuum, of course, because it was so much more pertinent to present himself as a perfect Roman hero if he had something against which to contrast himself. Antony was to provide him with an ideal antithesis. Octavian deliberately chose to adopt sober Roman attitudes and behaviour, and sober gods to promote his cause like Apollo and Mars. He referred to ancient Roman custom all the time, and as an additional insurance policy he began to imbue all his actions with glory, not for himself but for the people of Rome, whose saviour he was determined to become. The comparison with Antony played into his hands at every turn. In 37 Antony was the strongest of the Triumvirs, his military reputation was unsullied, and he had done nothing to incense the people against him. He had not descended on Italy to put himself at the head of the state, he had not forcefully evicted Italian landowners and tenants in order to settle his veterans. He had assisted Octavian whenever he was asked to do so, and he was preparing for an eastern campaign which promised to bring wealth, booty and vengeance for Rome. But there were already several loopholes for Octavian to exploit. Antony espoused eastern rather than Roman customs. His name was linked with the dangerous and scheming Queen of Egypt. He was, and had always been, far from sober himself, and he adopted far from sober gods such as Dionysus and Hercules to promote his cause. The rot had already set in as far as the Romans were concerned, and though it may have been subtle at first, easily remedied if only Antony could achieve a great victory against the Parthians, the fact that all these characteristics were deeply embedded and of long duration made it so much easier for Octavian to discredit him properly when the time came.

Antony chose to spend the winter of 37-36 not in Athens this time, but in Antioch in Syria, where he could gather information, issue orders more rapidly, and make preparations for the next spring. He left his family in Italy, preferring not to expose them to the dangers of the war zone. There was every excuse, since Octavia and Antony already had an infant daughter, the elder Antonia born in 39, and Octavia was pregnant for the second time; this child would be another daughter, Antonia *minor*, to distinguish her from her elder sister. Octavia had four children in her brood, since she had taken under her wing Antony's two sons by Fulvia, Antyllus and Iullus Antonius. In order to keep them safe, and perhaps to remind the people of Rome that he was still a

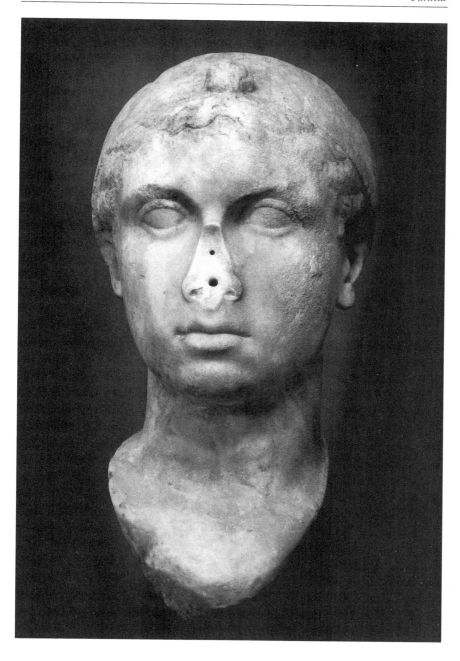

19.   *Head of Cleopatra, once again unadorned, but the features are more regular and quite bland compared to the head portrayed in Fig. 5.*

Courtesy Vatican Museums, Vatican City

force to be reckoned with, he insisted that the whole family should wait for him in Rome. Once he was free of them, he lost no time in inviting Cleopatra to Antioch to stay there with him until the campaign began. She brought with her the twins born to him in 40, Alexander Helios and Cleopatra Selene, who were now about three or four years old, and named for the sun (Helios) and moon (Selene). The names were not given to the children as the result of a whim or a fortuitous accident. They were meant to convey regal if not imperial authority. Antony acknowledged paternity of these two children. It may be that he married Cleopatra according to Egyptian rites, while they were at Antioch. The date and even the existence of any form of marriage between Antony and Cleopatra is disputed, and all the possible permutations have been proposed. Perhaps there was some form of ceremony at some time, either in Antioch or in Egypt, that could be construed as a marriage by eastern witnesses. There was the ready comparison with the gods, of a marriage between Osiris and Isis, or Dionysus and Aphrodite, which appealed to both Egyptian and Greek elements of the east. Alternatively there may have been no ceremony at all, but only an ongoing relationship, in which neither party cared about marriage as such. Whatever the truth of the affair, Octavian was able to make it seem that Antony had married Cleopatra illegally, since marriage with foreigners was forbidden by Roman law. An easterner could accept these ideas of a marriage between peoples of different races and backgrounds more readily than a Roman, so the contrivance of posing as Osiris and Isis, naming the children for the sun and moon, was double-edged; in the east Antony's actions in acknowledging these two children by Cleopatra would strengthen their joint authority, but in Rome it condemned him. Perhaps he knew what the result would be, but by now he did not care. It is possible to construe his behaviour in 37 as evidence that he had reached an irrevocable turning point, and had decided that if his future lay exclusively in the east, then he may as well eschew half measures, and in modern parlance, go for it, in full. He may have needed Egyptian wealth and support for his Parthian campaign, but he could have acquired all that without inviting the Queen to Antioch for the winter, and he certainly did not need to take her to bed and produce another child, who was born in the following year and named Ptolemy Philadelphus.

Cleopatra was not simply a personal guest, brought to Antioch for Antony's amusement for the months before he went to war. The Queen of Egypt was granted lucrative territories to add to her already wealthy domains. She ruled Crete, Cyrene and Cilicia, Phoenicia, and Nabataean Arabia. Most of these areas yielded profitable resources for Egypt. She was also given the balsam groves of Jericho, strictly part of the kingdom that Herod was winning back for himself. As business woman, Cleopatra was shrewd and ruthless, perhaps without equal in the ancient world, though of course there were probably many more women like her whose exploits have gone unrecorded. Herod was in no position to argue, having only just asserted his authority over Judaea, and disposed of the Parthian sympathiser Antigonus. Cleopatra leased the balsam groves back to him at a vast annual rent.

Antony supported Herod as king of Judaea, and reorganised the other eastern kingdoms to the advantage of Rome and naturally to his own satisfaction. The men he chose would serve Rome well, wisely changing sides when it was evident that Octavian was going to win the war and Antony was the loser. Treachery to Antony does not enter the picture; he would be the first to agree that when all else was lost, survival of the people and kingdom ought to be the first concern of any king. He reorganised some boundaries and refashioned some of the lesser kingdoms, choosing men whom he trusted for the larger territories. Galatia was entrusted to Amyntas, Polemo was installed as king of Pontus, and Archelaus was given Cappadocia instead of Antony's previous mistaken choice of Ariarathes. Before he embarked on his Parthian war, he ensured that he was surrounded by capable men who were as reliable as any man could be in the circumstances.

There remained the kingdoms outside his immediate control. During the period of preparation for the war, Antony sent Canidius Crassus to Armenia, to secure the territory for Rome. It was vital to neutralise this kingdom before marching into Parthia, so that the Roman army would not be faced with the possibility of an attack on their rear while they marched, or being cut off from their retreat. Canidius defeated Artavasdes, who obligingly severed his long-standing alliance with Parthia, and became the ally of Rome. But the victory brought further complications, since it rendered the neighbouring kingdom of Media nervous and hostile to Rome. It was well nigh impossible to be the friend and ally of both these mutually inimical kingdoms of Armenia and Media, so a choice had to be made between them. The king of Media, also called Artavasdes, strengthened his alliance with Parthia, but that was only to be expected. Military conquest was the only solution, but that would be left until the following year. Satisfied with the results in Armenia, Canidius went on to campaign against the peoples of the Caucasus. The first stage of the project was in operation, and so far it looked like standard Roman procedure for protecting the rear and flank of the invading army.

The timing of the Parthian war was only slightly faulty. If Antony could have started a year earlier he might have caught the enemy off guard. There had been a revolution in the ruling house, which had lasting consequences. The Parthian king Orodes was supposedly devastated by the death of his son Pacorus at the hands of Ventidius' army, so he abdicated in favour of one of his many other sons, Phraates. Shortly afterwards, Orodes died, or perhaps more likely he was killed on the orders of Phraates. All the many sons of Orodes and any other close relatives who might have posed a threat to Phraates also disappeared, including Phraates' own son. The eradication of opposition was not limited to the ruling house. Phraates went on to weed out suspect members of the nobility as well, much as the Triumvirs had rooted out opposition in Rome. Sadly, by the time that Antony invaded, Phraates had consolidated his position, and the comparative weakness of the Parthian high command could not be exploited to the full.

Antony's choice of Antioch as his winter quarters made it quite clear that his next project would be to invade Parthia. The eyes of many people in both the Roman and the Parthian worlds would be upon him. It was probably not his intention to keep the projected invasion secret, which would have been almost impossible to achieve, since at some point he would have to assemble troops and supplies somewhere near the border, for Parthian spies and sympathisers to observe and report on. Instead of preparing with the greatest secrecy, Antony made a noise about the forthcoming campaign. He sent an embassy to Phraates to ask for the return of the Roman standards lost at Carrhae. Presumably he did not expect that the request would be answered by the meek delivery of a bundle of Roman eagles accompanied by a note saying sorry. It was a declaration of intent, outlining the purpose of the coming war. The literary references to Antony's request for the return of the eagles would have deep significance for Augustan and later audiences, who would know perfectly well that, where Antony had failed, Augustus succeeded. In his early campaigns in Illyricum, before he was known as Augustus, Octavian retrieved the standards lost by Gabinius in the 40s. Then, as Augustus, without recourse to arms and without shedding any more Roman blood, he achieved the impossible. In 20, after a tense interlude of negotiating, the standards were returned to Rome by the Parthians. The contrast with Antony's military expedition and Augustus' diplomatic coup in 20 would render Antony that much more pathetic, all bluster, armed force and failure as against Augustus' cool, rational patience. The point is worth labouring, because Augustus laboured it himself. Literary references to the achievement leave no doubt as to its importance, and artistic representations on coins and statues were used to impress contemporaries and keep the tradition alive for posterity. The scenes depicted on the cuirass of the statue of Augustus from Prima Porta are all concerned with this event, and show the Parthian king humbled before the Roman Imperator. Where Antony could not prevail, Augustus triumphed. With this in mind, it is worth enquiring whether any of the stories of Antony's Parthian expedition are true. They may have been shaped and pruned to represent a greater fiasco than existed in reality. The few details derived from the ancient authors must be treated with caution.

Antony assembled troops at Zeugma on the north-eastern border of Syria, which served to draw the Parthian army into the plains of Mesopotamia to await his invasion. It was all very plausible, because to the east of Zeugma lay

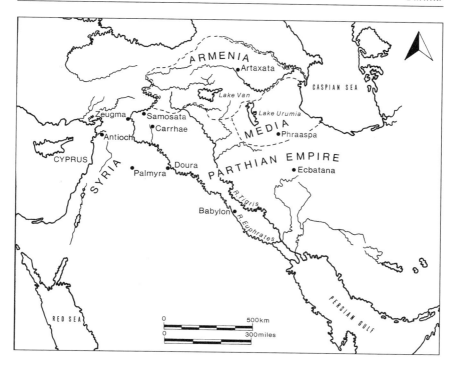

20.   *Antony's eastern campaigns. The Parthians invaded Syria in 40-39, but were driven out by Ventidius, who besieged the last remaining fugitives in Samosata. During the offensive against Parthia in 36, Antony assembled his troops at Zeugma as though he wished to invade Mesopotamia from the west, but then he marched rapidly north eastwards then south into Media, finally arriving at Phraaspa, to which he laid siege. If he had been successful, he would probably have marched on Ecbatana, the Parthian capital, but with the loss of his siege engines he had little chance of bringing the war to such a rapid close. When he prepared for the abortive campaign of 33, he had overrun Armenia and converted it into a Roman province, and forged an alliance with Media, so he perhaps planned to invade from the west from Syria and from the north from Media.*

Drawn by Graeme Stobbs

119

Carrhae, where Crassus had met defeat, so it would seem likely that the Romans were about to launch a grand campaign to avenge Crassus in the very place where he had died. But Antony did not enter Mesopotamia from Syria. Instead he marched north to Samosata and then by way of Armenia to Media, where he laid siege to the Median capital Phraaspa. The exact name of the city is not established. It is sometimes rendered as Phraapa; Plutarch calls it Phraata. The location is not known for certain, either. It may have been situated south-east of lake Urmia. Antony arrived there, despite the extremely long journey, before the Parthians did. It is said that Antony made it known that he was following a plan that Caesar had outlined long before. It is true that there would have been plenty of opportunity for Antony to discuss with Caesar where Crassus had gone wrong, in mistakenly fighting in the open plain against an enemy who excelled in that style of combat. There is of course no absolute proof that Antony ever said that he had access to Caesar's plans. It is not even certain that Caesar had made any plans, and it could be said that it was highly unlikely that he had revealed them to anyone. But the elaborate ruse to lure the enemy to a false battle ground and then the rapid dash to come down behind the Parthians was a typically Caesarian manoeuvre, risking all on speed and expertise. It might have succeeded. But it did not.

Antony dashed to Phraaspa without his siege train, which lumbered on behind him, protected by two legions under Oppius Statianus, some Pontic troops under their king Polemo, and contingents of Armenian troops recruited from Artavasdes. These fled when the Parthians attacked, Polemo was captured, but ransomed later, and Statianus was killed. Antony's siege train was destroyed. In itself it did not necessarily presage disaster. If Antony could reduce Phraaspa very quickly, he would be able to send the winter there and go on to attack Parthia itself in the next year. He may have intended to do so all along, but no-one knows what his plans were. It would make sense to reduce Media first, garrison it securely, and then make for the Parthian capital of Ecbatana. Events did not turn out that way, whatever Antony had planned, because Phraaspa did not fall to him. In the intervening period, the Parthians had arrived, and lingered just out of reach, harrassing Antony's army, but not giving battle. Despite all Antony's attempts to bring them to battle, and despite his considerable successes against the Parthian attacks on his besieging army, final victory eluded him.

When he was forced to the realisation that he had failed, he had to begin to think of retreat. With winter approaching, he could not continue the siege without doing irreparable harm to his army. If he could not inflict a decisive defeat on the Parthian army before winter came, it was very likely that his troops would be picked off little by little over the winter. The allies who marched confidently with him at the outset of the campaign would have no reason to remain with him, and could prove his undoing. He had gambled and lost and now he had to retreat. The Parthians for their part were worried that their allies might desert them, and go home to gather their crops if the siege went on too long, so Phraates had every reason to encourage Antony to retreat. He offered a truce; Antony asked for the return of the Roman standards; Phraates destroyed some of Antony's siege works, then offered a safe passage back to Armenia. If Antony believed that, he deserved no credit at all.

Plutarch describes how Antony had no heart for a speech to the soldiers announcing his decision, so he asked Domitius Ahenobarbus to make one. The soldiers for the most part understood why he had done so, and followed him loyally. As in any famous retreat, there were desperate heroics and tragedies. The Armenian contingents, whose heart was not in the campaign anyway, went home. Antony was left with an ever-reducing army, retreating over ground that had already been stripped of supplies, with the winter already advanced. He had been in this desperate position before when he left Mutina to march into Gaul, and in these difficult circumstances he once again showed himself capable, brave and resourceful. He used every stratagem that he had learned, so that Plutarch's account reads like a military manual on what to do when retreating, hard pressed by the enemy in difficult terrain. Discipline had to be enforced when the Romans wavered, so five days into the retreat, Antony decimated cowardly troops and put the survivors on punishment rations of barley instead of wheat. Unfortunately Plutarch does not enlighten his readers on where the supplies were obtained. At this point food was perhaps not in quite such short supply; later, the position would become desperate, so that the men ate roots of all descriptions, including one which caused madness. The victims started to turn over stones as though they had no other purpose in life, then eventually vomited and died. The antidote to the poisonous roots was said to be wine, but the Romans had long since run out of wine.

Training and expertise still existed in Antony's army, so that he was able to march in square formation, escorted by clouds of scouts and flanked by skirmishers. Even so, he lost many men, especially during an attack on the rearguard when according to Plutarch Antony lost 3000 dead and 5000 wounded. Progress was no doubt very slow. It is said that the army reached Armenia in 27 days, but even then the problems were not over. Antony was not capable of making any demonstration of strength in Armenia, though he was urged by the soldiers to take revenge on Artavasdes for deserting them. There was nothing to be gained from engaging in another war at the moment, but Antony would not forget.

It was time to act decisively to save what he could of his army. Domitius Ahenobarbus and Canidius were charged with bringing it out of the snows of Armenia, while Antony went on ahead to make arrangements for supplies of food and clothing. He made for the coast of Syria, and camped at a place called

Leuke Come, between Berytus and Sidon. He had sent messages to Cleopatra to bring food, clothing and money. Loyally, she set sail, risking a winter voyage, bringing with her the necessary supplies. It was probably in January 35 that she arrived there. While waiting for her, Antony took heavily to drink, more so than usual, if the reports are correct. Having nothing much to do, he kept leaping up from half-eaten meals to go outside, gazing wistfully seawards, hoping that her ships would appear on the horizon. It must have been a relief when they did. Antony set about distributing money, food and clothing to his soldiers, and after doing all that he could for their comfort, he went back with Cleopatra to Alexandria.

It was much more of a relief that the Parthian army did not follow him to Syria. He was not yet in a position to repel an invasion. Fortunately for Antony, the dissensions of the Parthian royal house prevented Phraates from mounting an aggressive campaign, and he was further restricted by the defection of Media. The two kings had quarrelled initially about the distribution of the Roman booty after Antony had retreated. The Median Artavasdes, recently Antony's enemy, made friendly overtures to him in 35, proposing dynastic marriage ties, and releasing the captive Polemo, king of Pontus. It was evident that there was more to the quarrel than the division of the spoils of war, and that here was an opportunity to exploit the differences of opinion to attack Parthia again. Instead of having to fight for and win a base, Antony could march into Media and pick up where he left off in winter 36. If he had grasped the opportunity there and then, he might have been able to achieve his aims, humble Parthia, retrieve the lost Roman standards, return them to Rome triumphant, and perhaps regain some of his lost supremacy in the west. But he could not reform his battle groups and begin again so early after the enervating retreat, and besides, there was another problem that he had to attend to first.

News reached Antony while he was in Syria that Octavian and Agrippa had finally defeated Sextus Pompey at the battle of Naulochus in early September 36. Agrippa had prepared thoroughly, building new ships to add to the depleted fleet, and training the crews for months on a lake, artificially deepened for the purpose, until they were more practised than Sextus' sailors. The battle had been won, and it gave control of Sicily, at last, to Octavian. It was an important province, because it yielded much of the corn that fed Rome. At this stage the corn supplies of Egypt were not under direct Roman control. The province had not fallen into Octavian's hands without a struggle, however. The forgotten Triumvir Lepidus had brought troops from Africa to help Octavian in the final land battles, and at their conclusion he had decided to assert himself, declaring Sicily his province and trying to hold it by force. His attempted resistance crumbled instantaneously. The result was that Octavian also gained control of Africa, another lucrative corn-producing area.

Lepidus was sent back to Italy and kept under surveillance for the rest of his life, for the next 24 years in fact. He was allowed to retain his priestly office as Pontifex Maximus, and when he died in 12 BC, Augustus as he then was quietly assumed the priesthood for himself. Patience was one of Octavian's enduring talents.

Antony perhaps did not mourn for the misfortunes of Lepidus, but he could not fail to take note of the significance of Octavian's steady encroachment of power. Very little stood in his way to sole power in Rome, except that Sextus Pompey was still at large. When all was lost at Naulochus, Sextus fled to the east, hoping for an alliance with Antony, which might have been arranged but for the fact that when he thought Antony had been defeated and possibly killed, Sextus did not wait to find out if the rumours were true, but began to intrigue with the Parthians. In all his dealings with Antony from then on Sextus showed himself to be thoroughly untrustworthy. Antony tried to be diplomatic, sending his general Titius against Sextus with orders to spare him if he submitted. The final encounter took place in Bithynia. Sextus began to recruit an army after landing at Nicomedia, drawing down on his own head the charge of outlawry. It was not clear what exactly he wanted, so no-one could take him on one side and give it to him; perhaps he did not know what it was himself. Some of Sextus' officers left him and joined Titius, intending to submit to Antony. Even then Sextus hoped to wriggle out of his predicament. He promised to negotiate, but only with Titius' colleague Furnius and king Amyntas of Galatia, not with Titius himself. While this was in the offing, Sextus then tried to burn some of Titius' fleet. His was a hopeless case, because he was, to use an anachronistic phrase, a loose cannon. In the end Amyntas captured him, and not wishing to compromise himself, he handed the renegade over to Titius, who executed him. Thus the last surviving son of Pompey the Great met his end. It was the only logical conclusion, so perhaps it does not really matter whether it was Titius who took the law into his own hands, or whether the final order came from Plancus, Antony's legate commanding Asia Minor and Syria.

The necessity of fighting a minor civil war, and perhaps sheer exhaustion, prevented Antony from taking any further action against Parthia in 35. He did not intend to remain entirely inactive, since he offered help to Octavian, who began a campaign against the tribes of Illyricum in that same year. More than ever, Octavian needed military renown and experience if he was ever to have full standing in Rome. Until now his victories had always depended on someone else, Antony at Philippi, Agrippa in Gaul and at Naulochus. As Caesar's son, he wanted to show that he too could wage successful wars and bring glory to Rome. More important still was the need for a legitimate excuse to keep an army together under his personal command. After his victory at Naulochus and the defeat of Lepidus, he had more than 40 legions at his disposal, far too many for the tasks in hand, but although he settled many of the veterans in the provinces, he still could not afford to disband all the troops. Antony had more than one reason to command a large army because without troops he could not administer and defend the eastern provinces, but once Sextus and Lepidus had been eliminated, Octavian could only reasonably command the armies in Gaul and Spain. If a future conflict with either Antony or even with the Senate were to develop, Octavian required more immediate access to troops than this would give him. Hence he conducted his campaigns in Illyricum, which were not strictly necessary for Rome's safety, and brought very little tribute into the coffers. But they did bring Octavian some credit, which he was quick to seize upon and enlarge. Antony's so-called Parthian victory was beginning to tarnish a little in the light of Octavian's more tangible successes.

This was the time when Antony should have gone to Rome to promote himself, while Octavian was engaged on his campaigns in Illyricum. He either chose not to go, or did not see the necessity of doing so. Even when his wife Octavia came to Athens with money, extra troops and supplies, he did not go to meet her, but directed her to send on the troops and to go back to Rome. His reasons are obscure, since he must have realised that this was a grave insult to a virtuous woman who had never done him any harm. Octavia dutifully returned to Rome, where she remained in his house looking after his children. She gained more credit by acting correctly and doing nothing than she would have done if she had wailed and protested. Antony's son Marcus Antonius Antyllus went to join his father in Alexandria, not necessarily as a result of any dispute with his step-mother, though there may have been some definite parting of the ways. Antony must have known that Octavian would eventually use his churlish behaviour against him, and perhaps intended to demonstrate to his colleague that he was now following an independent course. The ancient authors concluded that Antony was so besotted with Cleopatra that he no longer cared. The Queen of Egypt is blamed for the downfall of a once-mighty Roman general, using her wiles to enslave him each time he threatened to leave her. Plutarch even includes a ridiculous tale about her deliberate playacting to convince him that she was madly in love with him, greeting him with joy each time he appeared and not quite controlling her tears when he was absent. Not knowing what was in his mind, it is difficult to explain why Antony acted as he did. He is open to charges of stupidity, naivety, arrogance, misplaced confidence in his own abilities, or even madness. The incontrovertible fact is that when he repudiated Octavia so decisively in 35, he had burnt his boats. He may not have renounced Rome, but he had broken with Octavian. The final conflict had begun.

7 Prelude to war

Antony was consul in 34, but *in absentia* and only for one day. He laid down his powers and installed Lucius Sempronius Atratinus in his place. After a delay of one year, he intended now to settle accounts with Artavasdes of Armenia. It seems there were diplomatic exchanges to begin with, which yielded very little. Artavasdes refused family marriage ties with Antony and Cleopatra. Antony invited the Armenian king to join him in an expedition against Parthia. It was probably a ploy to test the Armenian king's mood, and to provide the excuse for either an alliance or an invasion. If Antony intended to launch another campaign against Parthia he needed to secure Armenia on a much more solid basis, even though it might take up valuable time. An ideal opportunity for another campaign had presented itself, since Phraates was deeply involved with his own dynastic squabbles with his family and his nobles, or what was left of them after his judicious disposal of the most troublesome elements. However much of this was known to the Romans and to the Armenian court, Artavasdes declined the invitation to join Antony's legions in another foray into Parthia.

Antony's response was to march to Nicopolis, a city founded by Pompey after his victories over Mithridates. The surviving story of Antony's Armenian campaign is suspect to say the least, because he is made to appear slipshod, disorderly, and devious. The whole episode is construed as a desire for revenge with no strategic purpose behind it, and even though there was a successful outcome from the Roman point of view, Antony's achievement is attributed to underhand activity and sheer luck, and any suggestion of military competence is obliterated from the record. It is probably true that Dellius was sent to negotiate with Artavasdes. That was after all Dellius' speciality. He had been sent to negotiate with Cleopatra when Antony summoned her to Tarsus, so it is to be expected that Dellius combined Roman authority with a certain amount of tactful deference. Perhaps, as Antony had expected, the negotiations failed, so the next step was to employ his troops to force Artavasdes to come to terms. Antony marched to Artaxata, where he invited Artavasdes to a conference. The king arrived and was promptly arrested with most of his family, put in chains, albeit made of silver, and sent to Alexandria as a prisoner. Roman garrisons were installed in Armenia. Shortly afterwards Antony returned to Alexandria, and issued coins bearing the legend *Armenia devicta*, or Armenia conquered. There is an element of ridicule in the story that has come down to us, no doubt inserted into the account by Octavian's propaganda, in order to diminish Antony's standing in Rome. In contemporary terms, Octavian could not afford to allow Antony to eclipse him. When he began to mobilise against him, it was in his interests to portray Antony as an incompetent villain, and to denigrate his eastern campaigns as purposeless failures. Even after his death there could be no slackening of the perception of Antony as corrrupt, even perverted, and there could certainly be no suggestion that he might after all have been a good general with a sound policy in mind when he invaded Armenia.

Yet the operation was probably not as ridiculous as it is made to seem. Simple revenge for the desertion of Artavasdes in the Parthian campaign will not suffice as the sole excuse for Antony's expedition. It was a costly enterprise and a long march, and was much more than a punitive campaign. The territory was overrun and converted into a Roman province, complete with military garrison and the rapid infiltration of Roman settlers and traders. Antony's claim to have conquered Armenia was perfectly correct, so Octavian could not deny it, but chose instead to cast doubt on the motives and methods that Antony used to achieve it. Treachery may have been the only way to capture Artavasdes, but there is no firm corroboration for the accusation, and if it is true, then at least Antony has no previous convictions on these charges. Conquest is not usually a gentle process whatever the circumstances and it cannot be said that the Romans were generally conscience stricken about the loss of life or the downfall of kings. The reason why Antony's campaign was depicted as useless and rather comic was doubtless because, far from being ill-advised, it promised to bring him success. He had prepared the ground for the last few years by installing independent but trustworthy rulers in the territories of the east, and two years after his disastrous defeat in Parthia he was ready to try again. With Armenia converted into a Roman province, his advance into Parthian territory would be greatly facilitated, and if he had to retreat again, then at least he would not have to march through a potentially hostile country once he had arrived at the border of Armenia. The next step was to ally with or perhaps invade the kingdom of Media. An alliance had already been proposed by the Median Artavasdes, and was now accepted. The king returned to Antony the captured standards of the two legions which had escorted the siege train during the invasion of 36. The daughter of Artavasdes was to be betrothed to Alexander Helios, and was brought to Alexandria in fulfilment of the alliance. Thus it was apparent that Antony was about to embark upon another Parthian campaign and this time, by dint of careful preparation, he might be successful. If so, his prestige in Rome would eclipse that of Octavian, and his power in the east would be immeasurably increased. His legions were prepared and in position for the projected invasion in the summer of 33. If Octavian was to stop him and prevent him from gaining tremendous credit as well as military power, then he had to do so very soon.

The Roman conquest of Armenia was thorough enough and would probably have fulfilled Antony's purpose, but it did not long survive him. During the civil war between Antony and Octavian, the Parthian court was embroiled in civil strife of its own, when Tiridates, perhaps a general in the Parthian army, ousted Phraates and drove him out of the kingdom. In the same year that Alexandria fell to Octavian, Phraates won his kingdom back again. Stronger than ever now, he also overran both Media and Armenia. There was no-one to stop his progress, so he installed Artaxes on the Armenian throne and probably rejoiced when the latter massacred all the Roman settlers and traders. Octavian, the victor of Actium and Alexandria, did not repair the damage by restoring Roman rule in Armenia. To have done so would have entailed embarking on a full-scale war with Parthia, so Octavian acquiesced in the loss of the territory, and Armenia reverted to an independent state on the borders of the Parthian and Roman Empires. If Octavian was to save face for not settling accounts with the Parthians and not putting a garrison back into Armenia, he was constrained to prevent any credit for the initial conquest from attaching itself to the name of Antony. He could not redress the balance, so what he could not obtain was presented as unworthy and unprofitable, and its original conqueror was depicted in the same light.

While Antony garrisoned Armenia, Octavian was fighting in Illyricum, making a name for himself as a general. These campaigns would have to be brought to a successful conclusion before he could turn his attention to Antony, but in the meantime his associates in Rome kept him in the public eye. Buildings, roadworks, policing for personal safety and security of property, provision of food and clean water, and the proper control of the sewage system of Rome all became the concern of Octavian and his colleagues. Agrippa had been given high office and independent commands, but now assumed the lowly role of aedile in 33 in order to inspect and repair the sewers and put in water pipes and fountains. Antony's generals also built temples and improved public facilities, but somehow their achievements were marginalised, outshone by everything that Octavian's men did. Sosius held a triumph in 34 for his exploits in the Jerusalem campaign when Herod won back his kingdom, but although Antonian generals featured almost as often as Octavian's men in the self-congratulatory military displays, collectively they were farther away and their achievements were not so carefully orchestrated. Even so, Antony may have succeeded in winning popular sympathy in Rome, but after the Armenian adventure he gave Octavian valid reasons to fear him, and also everything he required to present him as a threat to Rome.

21.   *Antony and Cleopatra on opposite sides of a silver denarius of 32. Antony makes the claim that he had conquered Armenia (ANTONI. ARMENIA. DEVICTA), a claim which Octavian decried as mere vacuous bluster, but which had some substance behind it since Armenia was garrisoned and opened up to Roman traders. Cleopatra staring grimly ahead emphasises Royalty as Queen of Kings and of her sons who are kings (CLEOPATRAE REGINAE REGUM FILIORUM REGUM). The message for Octavian was clear, that Caesarion was to succeed Cleopatra.*

© *British Museum*

When he returned to Alexandria in the autumn of 34, Antony paraded through the streets in a chariot, with his Armenian captives walking behind him. Cleopatra watched while seated high above the procession, with Caesarion at her side. It was too much like a parody of the Roman triumph for comfort, and though Antony probably had every right to do as he pleased, and may even have intended to provoke Octavian, the scenario as presented in Rome did him irreparable damage. It had sacrilegious undertones because the spoils of victory were traditionally dedicated to Jupiter Optimus Maximus, in his temple in Rome. Antony deprived the chief godhead of this privilege by staging his pseudo-triumph in a foreign city.

After the parade through the streets of Alexandria, either on the same day or a short time later, Antony and Cleopatra staged another ceremony which is known to historians as the Donations of Alexandria. Before a large gathering, seated next to Cleopatra on a high throne, with the children in front of them on smaller thrones, Antony redistributed territories, some of which were not yet conquered, to the immediate benefit of Cleopatra and her children. Alexander Helios was to rule Armenia, Media and Parthia, which was more a declaration of future intent rather than a true statement of the staus quo. Cleopatra Selene was to be ruler of Cyrenaica and Libya, and Ptolemy Philadelphus, aged about two, was given Syria and Cilicia. Antony did not set himself up as king in his own right, being content with his position as Roman Triumvir and commander of the east, but he was obviously playing the part of consort of the Queen of Egypt, and he now proclaimed that her son, the 13-year-old Caesarion, was the legitimate heir of Caesar. The coins that Antony issued proclaiming his Armenian conquests bore another message on the reverse with the legend *Cleopatrae reginae regum filiorum regum*, 'To Cleopatra, Queen of kings and of the sons of kings'. Antony publicly recognised Caesarion's claim to the throne of Egypt, which the boy currently shared with his mother Cleopatra and by implication would one day inherit as his sole preserve. This represented no little menace to Octavian, who was as far as he was concerned the only legitimate heir of Caesar. Thus far, however, the threat was purely personal, so it was not yet a cause which Octavian could realistically expect the whole of the Roman people to take up on his behalf. Egypt was not yet a Roman province, and Antony had not yet stepped too far outside the boundaries of Roman practice. If he went on to win a great victory in Parthia and settled the eastern frontier once and for all, the people of Rome would profit from the booty and the opportunities for settlement and trade, so they could afford to forgive Antony for his little lapse in Alexandria when he seemed to mock the Roman triumph.

There was a need for rapid conversion of Antony from potential hero to ominous enemy, so Octavian set about this task early in 33, as soon as the campaigns in Illyricum could be drawn to a happy conclusion. He embarked on a systematically organised crusade of abuse against Antony, launched by a speech in the Senate early in the year. He was consul in 33 and unassailable on account of his grant of tribunician sacrosanctity that was one of the rewards for his victory over Sextus Pompey in 36. He was not yet supreme in Italy, but he perhaps felt that there was no time to be lost in paving the way towards blackening Antony's name. His first speech would be a reliable test of the mood of the Senate and people of Rome, so he could estimate from its reception and the extent of the reaction how far he would have to go to achieve his aim. The timing of this inflammatory speech is not established beyond doubt and is consequently disputed. Some authors would place it at the beginning of 32, but it fits well with the situation in 33, when Antony was about to launch another attack on Parthia, and when the second term of the Triumvirate was coming to an end.

This too is the subject of considerable ongoing debate, because it is not known what exactly was agreed when the Triumvirate was renewed, and the sources contradict each other. Appian states that the Triumvirate was to be terminated at the end of 32, and some modern scholars agree, on the supposition that the second five-year term was dated from January 36. On the other hand it is possible to argue that if the new inaugural date really was 36, then the Triumvirate suffered a break between the end of 37 and the beginning of the following year, which some authorities find hard to accept, especially since Augustus himself declared in his *Res Gestae* written near the end of his life that he was Triumvir for ten consecutive years. While this implies that there was no break in 37-36, it could also refer to the fact that Octavian ceased to use the title Triumvir before the agreement came to an end, whereas Antony used it for much longer, perhaps exceeding the ten years that Octavian virtuously proclaimed. The truth cannot be established, but the broad general picture is clear. Soon, either at the end of 33 or one year later the Triumvirate would end, and Octavian was anxious to make an unequivocal statement that he did not intend to enter into another agreement with Antony.

The grounds for a personal break with Antony were already present in his treatment of his wife Octavia, a fact which Octavian used to his own advantage. This would incense the people, but might not move the Senate. It would have been tremendously difficult for Octavian if Antony had been detached and independent, acting purely as a Roman official at the head of Roman armies. In that case, Octavian would have had to employ even more unscrupulous tactics to stir up feeling against him. Fortunately for his enemies, Antony had a long history of eastern associations and sympathies, a reputation for drunkenness and renegade social behaviour, and now an obvious affinity with the Queen of Egypt. It was upon Cleopatra that Octavian began to focus. Antony was the real object but it was much more acceptable and far more politically correct to instigate a war against a foreign enemy. Octavian had proclaimed an end to civil wars when he had defeated Sextus Pompey, so he would lose face now if he had to go back on his word and try to persuade the Roman people to embark on yet another civil war.

Something of the new feeling in Rome reached Antony while he was in Armenia in 33. He defended himself with a counterblast against Octavian that revealed that he had a firm grasp on political reality, much as he had shown himself fully aware of the situation when Cicero was stirring up hostility towards him before the battles of Mutina. Antony pointed out that Octavian had not returned the ships that he had borrowed before the battle of Naulochus, and he had not kept his word about the 20,000 soldiers that he was supposed to send as his part of the bargain. Belatedly taking up the cause of Lepidus, Antony castigated Octavian for his treatment of their third partner. Favourable publicity in Italy may have been one of the motives behind this accusation, since Lepidus had not been foremost on Antony's list of priorities until now. His veterans on the other hand were dearer to him, and he accused Octavian of partiality to his own veterans at the expense of Antony's troops. It may not have been true, but many people in Italy probably thought it was an accurate assessment, so Antony appealed to them when he protested about the situation in his letter. Reputedly he also blamed Octavian for not sharing Sicily with him. Here he was not standing on very firm ground. The story may be suspect, but it allowed Octavian to reply that he would partition Sicily just as soon as Antony partitioned Armenia and gave him half of it. In Rome this may have been seen as something of a joke, because Octavian had probably already portrayed the Armenian conquest as ridiculously easy and carried out by dubious and devious means.

Then the abuse became more personal. Octavian wrote to Antony reproaching him for his rejection of Octavia and his elevation of Caesarion, but most of all for his relationship with Cleopatra. Antony replied in kind, in a letter that is famously reproduced in Suetonius' life of Augustus. It is a crude soldier's letter, perhaps authentic, in which Antony says that sexual relationships do not really mean anything, since after all Octavian himself was known to have taken all sorts of women to bed, and as Antony goes on to say, 'Does it really matter where you get your erections?' But he also asks why there should be any surprise concerning Cleopatra, because '*uxor mea est*' which means literally 'she is my wife'. Convoluted theories have been proposed about this simple phrase. Those who do not believe that there was ever any form of marriage ceremony between Antony and Cleopatra are forced to the conclusion that this sentence ought to be converted into a question, so it can be rendered as 'Is she my wife?'. The implication would then be that it was perfectly acceptable for Antony to associate with Cleopatra and produce children by her, because he had not taken the final step of entering into a bigamous and foreign marriage. There were no helpful punctuation marks in the Latin which would settle the question once and for all. On balance, it is best to take Antony's statement at face value, since he could very easily have inserted '*non*' between '*mea*' and '*est*' to make himself crystal clear. Acceptance of his statement then involves recognition of the fact that he had damaged his reputation by this marriage, arranged while he was still married to Octavia and while he was perfectly aware that it was illegal for a Roman to marry a foreigner. This was a situation that Octavian could use against him to great advantage.

A war of words followed, with accusations winging their way between Rome and Armenia, but by itself that would not have been a cause for concern. It had happened before. What finally brought Antony out of Armenia before he had begun any military activity in the east was the realisation that Octavian had won over too many people and had probably brow-beaten the Senate into submission. Support in Rome was vital and Antony stood to lose too much if he allowed Octavian to go on alienating him. In the autumn of 33 he turned his face towards Rome and away from Parthia. He now had to win over the Senate to his side, and though he did not need to do so he began by asking for formal ratification of his acts in the east. It was a diplomatic move, because he had already secured ratification for everthing he had done and was likely to do before he left Rome in October 39. More importantly he offered to lay down his Triumviral powers if Octavian would comply and lay down his powers as well. It was Caesar and Pompey all over again, and people in Rome and Italy would have begun to feel very tense.

By November 33, Antony had bowed to the inevitable and started to prepare for war. He ordered the faithful Canidius to bring the army out of Armenia, and he began to assemble troops around his winter base at Ephesus. Cleopatra joined him there. Her resources in money, ships and manpower would be very necessary, so, when some of the Romans in Antony's army protested that she should be sent home to Egypt, Canidius for one countered that she had every right to stay, since she was paying the army. He was promptly accused of accepting bribes from the Queen to support her. The seeds of dissension were firmly planted and perhaps could not be eradicated at this stage. Everything that Octavian said about Cleopatra would henceforth find its mark not only at Rome but also in Antony's army, but Antony could not possibly break with her decisively and stand alone. If war were to be declared against either of them, Antony and Cleopatra would have to fight side by side, since neither of them could now hope for an independent reconciliation with Octavian.

At the beginning of 32, the Antonian generals Sosius and Domitius Ahenobarbus took up office as consuls. Theoretically, all should have gone well for Antony, but Octavian had been strengthening himself and was ready for any eventuality. The story goes that Antony had sent a despatch to his consuls to be read in the Senate but the two men decided that it was too infamous to be revealed. Among other things, it purported to outline the Donations of Alexandria, which strictly speaking could not possibly have been unheard of in Rome by this time. There is considerable doubt as to the authenticity of the tale; as it stands it condemns Antony for his character and behaviour, but in the absence of a fully documented description of the circumstances, it is open to speculation. Firstly it may not even be true, but might be a later shadowy interpolation to denounce Antony by vague but credible accusations against him. There is nothing so damning as unsubstantiated rumour, which can be embroidered, elaborated upon, and inflated according to the whims of the audience. Secondly, if it is true that Antony's letter contained information too dangerous to reveal to the Roman public in January 31, it attests to the effectiveness of Octavian's steady campaign against Antony, suggesting that he had whipped up feeling to flashpoint.

This is implied in the subsequent events. Octavian was not in Rome in February when Sosius made a speech denouncing him. If he did not dare to read out Antony's letter, Sosius apparently had enough courage to try to turn the tables on Octavian. It is not known what he said, but his speech may have reiterated something that Antony had pointed out in a letter to Octavian during their war of words in 33, namely that the major obstacle to the restoration of the Republic was Octavian himself and his single minded pursuit of power. Sosius probably asked the Senate to declare Octavian out of order, if not actually anything more serious. It is not generally suggested that he wished to declare Octavian an enemy of the state, and if there had been the merest suggestion of that, Octavian would have used it as the justification for the civil war. Whatever it was, the tribune Nonius Balbus vetoed the suggestion. No-one knows whether Nonius was in the pay of Octavian to protect his interests, or in the pay of the Antonians to rescue them from an impossible situation if the speech in the Senate went badly wrong. The meeting broke up inconclusively.

Octavian lost no time now. His position is unclarified. If the Triumvirate had indeed ended in December 33, then he had no legal office, and should not have been able to command troops. But the legal niceties were perhaps never fully investigated or elucidated. The realities of power were clear enough and were after all the only things that counted now. Returning to Rome with a bodyguard, Octavian convened the Senate, entered the meeting in force, and sat between the two consuls. It was undoubtedly illegal, but the time for propriety was long past and it was very effective. He said that he would bring documentary proof to the next meeting that would condemn Antony out of hand. No-one knows what this evidence was, and Octavian was never put to the test of producing it; the mere threat was sufficient. The result was pandemonium. The two consuls and many senators fled to Antony. It is said that 300 senators joined Antony, but the figure is only a guess, derived from the fact that Augustus later declared that 700 senators remained with him. The assumption is that the full Senate after Caesar had augmented it comprised 1000 members, therefore 1000 minus 700 equals 300, so that is the number that is thought to have gone to Antony at Ephesus.

On the face of it this immediate reaction was extreme, but there is no proper documentation of the background. Senators do not uproot themselves and sail to another part of the world because of a few speeches in the Senate House. They will have seen all the signs that are lost to a modern audience, and interpreted them correctly. Too many of them would remember the proscriptions of only a decade ago, when the world saw precisely how far both Octavian and Antony would go to gain their ends. To be caught in the cross-fire was not wise, and for some men neutrality would not be a viable option. That would be possible only if a long foundation of impartiality had already been laid. The choice was Octavian and war with Antony, or vice versa. There can be no record of what preceded these events because Octavian will have had a vested interest in obscuring the opening stages of the war. He had carefully engineered it for his own ends, so both for contemporaries and indeed retrospectively he had to make it seem that he was saving the state from a terrible menace. This menace was not specifically Antony but Cleopatra and the use to which she might put him. The vilification of the Egyptian Queen was actively pursued from now onwards. It was one way of unifying the opposition.

If the remaining senators needed any more urging to war, Octavian found the ideal tool. Sensing the way that the wind was blowing, Antony's generals Titius and Plancus deserted him and came to Octavian in Rome. They perhaps could not tolerate the close relationship of Antony with Cleopatra, or at least could not tolerate the way in which her continued presence played into Octavian's hands. Antony finally divorced Octavia in 32, so perhaps until that point the Romans in Antony's entourage could believe that he was still committed to her and perhaps to Octavian, with the Egyptian Queen as a profitable ally. More likely they simply wanted to survive and therefore had to be on the winning side, which they now calculated would be Octavian's. According to the legend, Titius and Plancus told Octavian that Antony had written his will and lodged it with the Vestals in Rome, as was the usual custom. Another variation on this tale is that it was with a friend of Antony's, but wherever it was, its location was revealed to Octavian, who immediately searched for it and opened it. This was one more fortunate opportunity to reveal to the Romans just how depraved Antony had become. The enormity of Octavian's action was perhaps overshadowed by what he found in the will, or said that he had found. He opened the will in private, but seemingly no-one accused him of forgery, of all of it, or parts of it. The sentiments expressed in the will were so plausible that perhaps no-one ever thought that they may not have been authentic. The main points in it were that Antony reaffirmed the legitimacy of the claims of Caesarion to be Caesar's son, and the co-ruler and heir to the Egyptian throne; he granted legacies to his children by Cleopatra, which meant that he acknowledged them as his own; he clearly intended Antyllus to be his own heir, and had issued coins with his own head and that of his son on them. The most damaging part of Antony's will was his obvious determination to remain with Cleopatra, even after death, for he asked that he should be buried alongside her in Alexandria. He seemed now to have renounced Rome altogether, but it was also implied that his schemes for world domination involved supplanting Rome in favour of the Egyptian city. It was rumoured that he was going to remove the seat of government there. The threat was enough to make the Romans clamour for war, in unified antagonism towards Cleopatra and her bewitched consort Antony.

In carrying that unity further afield, Octavian was more thorough, thus revealing the caution with which he laid his plans. He arranged that all of Italy should swear an oath of allegiance to him, with the exception of those towns where Antony had many clients, the chief of which was Bononia (modern Bologna). There were precedents for using the Italian towns to pressurise the Senate to act, as for instance when Pompey asked the municipalities to agitate for the recall of Cicero from exile. Octavian's use of the Italian municipalities was something different, in that what he extracted from them was an oath to a leader, not to Rome itself, and not to the Senate. It may have been the foundation of the oath sworn to each new Emperor, when the Empire had been firmly established, but in 32 it was quite novel. It gave Octavian the moral authority to act as he did against Cleopatra, quite separately from any legal command he might be given. Augustus stated in his *Res Gestae* that the oath was sworn spontaneously by all of Italy, which simple declaration belies a great deal of preparation and paper work, not to mention some little coercion.

The next problem was to declare war in a proper fashion. The excuse was that Cleopatra aimed at domination of the Roman world, and it seemed eminently plausible by now, so feelings ran high. It was therefore to be a just war, waged in self-defence, as all Roman wars were said to be, but there must be some ceremonial in declaring it. Octavian revived a very old ritual whereby a patch of earth was designated as enemy territory, and war was declared by the action of throwing a spear into it. Characteristically, Octavian appealed to the distant Roman past to give his actions an unassailable authenticity. It was to be a constant theme of his supremacy that he modernised the Roman world only within the framework of ancient tradition, unsullied by foreign values or practices. That was where Antony had gone wrong, and his fate should be a lesson to all.

8 Decline and fall

Antony spent the winter of 32-31 at Patrae, on the north coast of Achaea, watching over the Gulf of Corinth. His troops were strung out along the coast of Greece from Corcyra to Methone, with the largest number camped near the Gulf of Ambracia. Two peninsulas like encircling arms guarded the narrow channel into the waters of the gulf. Antony's men watched the entrance from the southern peninsula, on the Actian side. Antony had built up a huge fleet of about 500 ships, perhaps the largest that had ever operated in one war. He had about 11 legions, though Plutarch says that he had 16; they were not all at full strength, but he had also recruited native levies, especially cavalry, so in terms of numbers he had no serious worries. He had organised food depots and his naval communications were good, but he had to guard the long craggy coast of Greece with all its inlets and landing places. That was to prove an impossible task, and naturally reduced the number of ships and personnel at his disposal at the battle of Actium.

Antony had probably decided against repeating the pattern of the two previous civil wars, where battles were fought on land. He clung to the coast and did not withdraw into Macedonia, nor did he really pay much attention to the hinterland. Consequently he had little or no communication with the land to the rear of his army, but instead faced resolutely and exclusively westwards. He has been accused of putting the security of Egypt before everything else, or even worse, it has been suggested that he was primarily concerned for his own and Cleopatra's personal safety. The ancient sources for the campaign strategy and the battle of Actium are meagre, which leaves many questions unanswered. High-sounding literature about it abounds, but it is retrospective and laudatory, epoch-making in intent and quite out of proportion with the actual events. It seems that there was no heroic battle but a series of skirmishes on land and a few exchanges at sea. Antony is portrayed almost as a man in a dream, completely unable to develop or carry out a plan.

From the evidence of the ancient writers, if what has come down to us can be called evidence, it is not feasible to reconstruct a coherent account of the campaign. It was a long and drawn-out affair lasting for several months, but

22   *Antony issued vast amounts of legionary coins, naming his legions individually.*
      This silver denarius of 31 depicts the standards of the Seventh legion (Legio VII)
      on the reverse, while Antony on the obverse reminds his soldiers that he is still
      Triumvir, though by now Octavian had ceased to use this title.

© *British Museum*

only some disconnected details are known. Antony did not use his fleet to engage Octavian at sea while he crossed from Italy in the spring of 31, but allowed him to sail unopposed from Brundisium across the Adriatic, and land most of his army not far from the point where Caesar disembarked in 48. Octavian's army and the fleet then progressed southwards down the coast, and Octavian himself was able to set up a base at Corfu, because the Antonian ships had withdrawn from the island. Quite rapidly, Octavian arrived at the northern peninsula of the Gulf of Ambracia. His first thought would have been to try to gain control over the mouth of the gulf, but it was too well defended by Antony's troops. Octavian moved off further up the northern peninsula and dug in at Mikhalitzi. It may have been part of Antony's plan to lure him to the gulf, so that he could choose the battle ground himself, but if so he gained no advantage from it. Antony and the bulk of his army joined the troops on the southern peninsula, made camp and almost immediately afterwards crossed the mouth of the gulf with the allied cavalry and some of the legionaries to try to cut off Octavian's camp from its water supply, but the attack failed, because Antony's native troops deserted to Octavian. A second attempt, led by Antony in person also failed because this time even Amyntas, who had been made king of Galatia thanks to Antony, went over to Octavian. Presumably very dispirited, Antony ferried his troops back over the entrance to the gulf and camped once again on the southern peninsula. The narrative sounds suspiciously simple, as though everything that Antony did was a

23   *An optimistic portrayal of the goddess Victory and the head of the god Jupiter Ammon, an amalgamation of the chief Roman god with his eastern counterpart. These silver denarii were issued by Antony and his general Scarpus in 31. The legend round the head of Jupiter Ammon runs M. ANTONIO. COS III. IMP.IIII, proclaiming that Antony was consul for the third time in 31. This was not strictly true. He had been designated consul, but Octavian deprived him of his office. The abbreviated IMP.IIII indicates that Antony had been hailed as Imperator by his troops for the fourth time, the context for which must be 31, so his performance during the land battles at Actium was probably not as miserable as the ancient sources suggest.*

© British Museum

supreme failure, but coin evidence shows that at some point he was hailed as Imperator for the fourth time in his career, which means that he did enjoy at least one victory. The context is not known but it perhaps suggests that the attempt to blockade and cut off Octavian's camp was not such a shambles as it has been described. There may have been some hard fighting which Octavian would rather forget. One of the main problems is that there is no properly established chronology for the whole campaign, and only Octavian's successes are elaborated upon. Antony's little excursion across the gulf is made to seem transitory and wasteful.

Agrippa commanded Octavian's fleet, very practised and confident after the victory at Naulochus four and a half years earlier. He used it to good effect, first capturing Methone and gaining a base in the Peloponnese, and then going on to annihilate the Antonian ships at Leucas. Shortly afterwards he took Patrae and then Corinth. This left the fleet free to block the mouth of the Gulf of Ambracia, where Antony's ships were bottled up. Sosius tried to break out with at least a part of the Antonian fleet, but he was defeated and driven back.

Thus from the landward side and then from the sea Agrippa and Octavian were able to tighten the circle around Antony, creating considerable difficulties for him in receiving supplies. Octavian meanwhile built two walls from his camp to the sea, and thereby secured his own supplies.

Antony's most pressing need at the opening of the campaign was for a quick victory over Octavian, either on land or over the fleet. Once he had lost the initiative, he also seems to have lost the momentum. He needed to bring Octavian to battle, and perhaps stayed too long in trying to force the issue. By remaining at Actium instead of marching away and making Octavian follow or wait for him to come back, Antony had sealed his own doom. The position of his camp was not very salubrious, and his troops began to fall sick. Supplies were short, and there was no fodder. Malaria and dysentery caused havoc as the hot weather arrived, and morale plummeted to rock bottom. More of Antony's once-trusted officers deserted him, including even Domitius Ahenobarbus and Dellius. The demoralising effect must have been tremendous.

The reasons for the continual desertions have not been elucidated in great detail. The allied levies of infantry and cavalry may have been subverted by Octavian long before he arrived at Actium. Dio indicates that spies were active on both sides before the war started in earnest, and Antony sent money far and wide to recruit people to his cause. Octavian found out and redoubled his own efforts, but he was presumably already doing exactly the same thing in the east. Inscriptions such as those from Aphrodisias show that Octavian was no stranger to the cities of the east, and that he could give what amounted to direct orders to them without reference to Antony. In that case he would have found it reasonably easy to infiltrate the consciousness of the ruling classes of several cities and states via his agents. How the various kings and high officials viewed him would depend very much on his successes at Rome and in his Illyrian campaigns, and very much more on his own self-promotion and the amounts of money he could offer them. He would need to convince them that he was the eminently dependable man, whiter than white, who could guarantee and support their future prosperity and security. One of the principal tools that he used in Rome was fear and loathing of Cleopatra, and he no doubt harped on the same theme in the east. It would be easy enough to keep agents on his payroll to whisper into the ears of Antony's allies, and the petty kings and noble rulers whom he had set up, that their future survival may be threatened if Antony succeeded in subduing Parthia and still kept up his association with Cleopatra. The Queen's track record so far would only support the suspicions. She had milked the prosperous areas of the east for whatever she felt that Egypt needed, and she had a blatant influence over Antony. The Donations of Alexandria would have been viewed by the eastern kings and princes with great suspicion, especially since there were already five offspring on whom it was likely that Antony would bestow further kingdoms, and it was quite possible that more children, all potential monarchs, might be born in the future. The fact that Antony had not succumbed to all Cleopatra's demands would carry no weight at all once the initial misgivings were planted in men's minds. It had been remarked that after Actium and the fall of Alexandria, Octavian turned his full attention to the east, but made few changes to the arrangements and dispositions that Antony had made. One reason is undoubtedly that Antony had been eminently sensible in his choice of rulers and officials, and had reorganised territorial boundaries with intelligence. Another reason might be that Octavian had already had some long-standing dialogue with these rulers before he annihilated Antony, offering them as their rewards continued unassailable sovereignty in their domains. All he had to do was to convince them that there was a real danger of territorial encroachment by Cleopatra, and then promise to protect them from it. Thus the oaths of loyalty that the allies swore to Antony in 31 were probably empty promises from the very beginning.

The Roman officers and senators who deserted to Octavian may have entertained the same fears once they saw Cleopatra in action. It is possible that they arrived on the scene with stories and rumours embedded in their minds that they were prepared to doubt, but then they would find that some of the tales were true. Even if they merely saw the innocuous traits, it would set them wondering if the more damaging stories may also be true. After the serious desertions of men like Dellius and Domitius Ahenobarbus had begun, the remaining officers would feel very nervous. Antony further alienated both his allies and his senatorial colleagues by torturing Iamblichus, the king commanding his Arabian contigents, and by executing the senator Quintus Postumius. It may have been necessary to assert himself and try to restore discipline, but the effect on those still with him would only have been to increase their doubts about whether they were on the right side in this war.

Canidius remained, and in a meeting of the high command he voted for a retreat eastwards into Macedonia, and then fighting a land battle, but that meant abandoning the huge fleet. Cleopatra was determined to use it, so the vote went her way, and Antony committed himself to a naval battle. It is said that he ordered the crews to take their sails with them, and that he also put on board his treasure chests, which to many men signified the possibility that he intended to break out and sail away rather than to fight a proper battle. Another possible explanation for the sails is that Antony intended to make use of the freshening winds that usually blew up in the afternoons to enable him to get round Agrippa's fleet and turn it. If he could do that he would be able to cut the fleet off from the shore and separate it from Octavian's army, and perhaps roll it up by sheer weight of numbers, drawing the net all around it.

The weather was too unsettled to carry out this or any other plan until 2

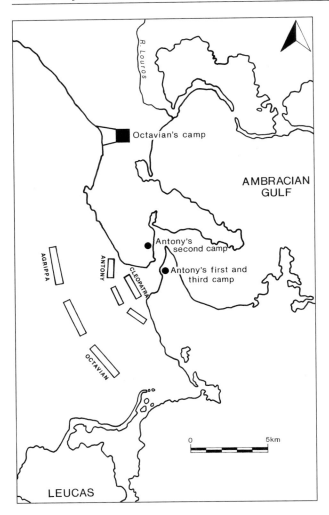

24. *The battle of Actium, 2 September 31. Before the naval battle was fought, there was a prolonged series of skirmishes on land, which cannot be documented in detail. Antony crossed the entrance to the Gulf of Ambracia to try to cut off Octavian's water supply, but he had to withdraw as his allies deserted him. Octavian built protective walls from his camp to the sea to ensure his uspplies, and meanwhile Agrippa captured several ports and harbours, including the island of Leucas to the south of Actium. As the stranglehold on Antony grew more serious, he was forced to try to break out. Instead of retreating into Macedonia as Canidius advised, he chose to fight at sea. Many of his ships turned back into harbour, while he and Cleopatra sailed away to Egypt.*

Drawn by Graeme Stobbs

September, when there was a calmer interlude in the morning. Antony came out in strength, putting himself and his flagship on his right, with which he tried to turn Agrippa's left. The two lines held their positions for a while, rowing now and then to keep their places. Agrippa made no move to close with Antony, so eventually the latter had to make a choice, to attack or to return to harbour. He moved forward with the right, leaving the slower centre behind. The race was now on, with the two lines of Agrippa's left and Antony's right gradually stretching out, each trying to outdo the other. They engaged quite fiercely and there were losses on either side. Then in the rear, some of Antony's ships turned and went back into harbour, and Cleopatra, perhaps ordered to do so, turned southwards, which left Antony's right unsupported and hard pressed. His own ship was in the thick of the fighting, and when the time came to escape he could not safely disengage. He left the flagship and transferred to a smaller craft, and then to Cleopatra's ship. In all, out of about 500 ships, he escaped to Egypt with perhaps less than 100. It is hardly surprising that Octavian made such mileage out of the story.

Though the battle was over, as so often, the war was not yet won. Like Pompey after the battle of Pharsalus, Antony could regain his strength, and regroup his army, which Canidius led by land from Greece to Egypt. But that required energy, and from the moment when Antony transferred to Cleopatra's ship, his determination evaporated. Except for the duration of the brief attack by Octavian's pursuing ships, which he successfuly averted, Antony spent the entire voyage of three days in the bows of the ship, silent and probably beyond words. He had known defeat before, but had always revived his own and his soldiers' spirits, and emerged fighting fit, ready for anything, without losing credibility or the faith of the army. This time he offered his friends money and the means of escape, which indicates that he thought his cause was lost, and he did not want to bring his friends down with him. By now he was becoming accustomed to desertions, so perhaps he wanted to pre-empt any further disappointment by weeding out those who wished to leave before he reached Egypt. He could not know it yet, but Canidius' troops were subverted by Octavian's messengers, who caught up with them on their march. Mindful only of their own fate, the soldiers wrangled for profitable terms for seven days and eventually Octavian agreed to all that they asked. Negotiation was better than fighting unnecessarily, as both sides knew perfectly well, and Octavian gambled on making promises now and trying to fulfil them later. Canidius refused to join Octavian, and went on to join Antony in Egypt. His loyalty ensured that when Octavian caught up with him again, he received no mercy. Hopefully, Antony appreciated the qualities of this loyal officer.

Approaching the coast of northern Africa, Antony and Cleopatra could not be certain of their reception in Egypt. They landed first at a small harbour far

25.   *Relic of the battle of Actium. This* rostrum *made of bronze was fixed to the prow
of a galley to strengthen it when ramming enemy ships.*

© British Museum

to the west of Alexandria, while they sounded out the state of affairs in the city,
which was calm and ready to receive the Queen, and whether the legions of
Cyrenaica were still favourable to Antony. They were not. Cleopatra sailed
back to Alexandria, where she quickly asserted herself. There was no hint of
the defeat at Actium as she entered the city; her ships were decorated for
victory, and her demeanour was not subdued. She executed Artavasdes of
Armenia, which would serve to secure the loyalties of his rival Artavasdes of
Media. For a while, Antony remained in the western desert. His state of mind
can only be guessed. He was perhaps suicidal, as Plutarch says. If he
contemplated ending it all he did not go through with it, and finally went back
to Alexandria to join Cleopatra.

It was certain that Octavian would eventually bring the war to Egypt, so
there was much to be done before he arrived. Antony probably had little to
hope for except survival, his dreams of Empire, if he had ever entertained any,
shattered with the failure at Actium. He had lost heart for the struggle for
mastery of Rome, if indeed he had ever entertained any ambition for sole rule.

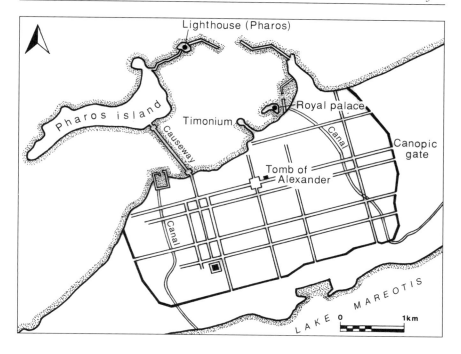

26.   *Plan of Alexandria showing the location of the Royal Palace and the Timoneum where Antony withdrew after Actium.*

Drawn by Graeme Stobbs

He built himself a little retreat on the shoreline, and called it the Timoneum, after Timon of Athens, whose claim to fame was his rejection of humanity and his life as a hermit. Cleopatra had now to defend her kingdom and her children, as well as her own life, by her own efforts. She did what she could to organise a united defence, presenting Caesarion to the people as Ptolemy XV, and at the same time Antyllus was recognised as an adult, by the Roman ceremony of assuming the *toga virilis*, exchanging his boy's clothing for the dress of a man. The purpose of declaring the two boys the adult heirs of the Queen of Egypt and her consort Antony was probably to foster the appearance of continuity, to give the impression that she thought there was a future to plan for. She tried to revive Antony by the usual methods — parties, drinking, and late night revels. He joined in, but the Society of Inimitable Livers was replaced now by the Inseparables at Death. His attitude was justifiable. He had pared down his associates to those who would perhaps remain with him, and he knew that this time it would be to the bitter end, which he anticipated would probably not be long in coming.

145

Octavian spent most of the winter on the island of Samos, interrupted by a hasty visit to Italy to settle disturbances there caused by the settlement of veterans. His friends Maecenas and Agrippa were unable to bring the situation under control. There was perhaps another problem. At some time which is not established beyond doubt, the younger Lepidus tried to raise revolt against Octavian on behalf of his father, who was still powerless and disgraced, living in enforced retirement on his estates. Some scholars prefer to date this event to the following year, and there is no way of proving whether it occurred before or after the fall of Alexandria. Whenever it happened, it is eloquent testimony to the fact that Octavian was not universally accepted in Italy or Rome, but it is also tesimony to the fact that he was powerful enough to end attempts at opposition quite smoothly.

During the winter, embassies sped back and forth between Octavian and Antony, and perhaps separately between Octavian and Cleopatra. It is said that Antony promised to do away with himself if Octavian would guarantee the safety of Cleopatra. If it is true, it shows that he had lost all hope, and was prepared to resort to noble and heroic gestures. Perhaps he thought that he was the main object of Octavian's crusade, and that once he was removed from the scene then Octavian could assume command of the entire Roman world. Indeed, Octavian corroborated this judgement by writing to Cleopatra, offering lenient terms if she would lay down her arms and surrender Antony. She refused, either because she loved Antony very deeply, as he perhaps loved her in offering his life for hers, or because they both knew that what Octavian really wanted was Egypt itself, and he meant to have it no matter that he might have to scramble over their dead bodies to get it. One of the greatest worries that beset Octavian was that Cleopatra might destroy all her treasure before he could seize it. He required astronomical sums of money to fulfil all the promises he had made to the soldiers and his allies, and control of the surplus food supply that Egypt could well afford would be of enormous advantage to him.

The country was united in its support of Cleopatra, and there were rumours of an uprising of the people on her behalf. She had always attended to the needs of the populace, to a far greater extent than the previous Ptolemies, and if she had given the word there would have been an army of common people, marching to Alexandria, ready to do her bidding. She refused the offer, because she did not want to involve her people in war. She guessed correctly that Octavian would leave the people to get on with their lives if he could divert the taxes and the surplus food into his own coffers.

In the spring of 30 Octavian was ready to carry the war into Egypt. He returned to Greece and marched overland, reaching his objective by July. Cleopatra sent her son Caesarion, now aged 16, on a journey up the Nile into Upper Egypt, perhaps intending that he should cross the Red Sea, or travel

27.   *Alexandria fell on 1 August 30. Three years later Octavian reminded the Roman world that he had captured Egypt, on this gold aureus of 27. He styled himself CAESAR. DIVI.F. COS. VII (Caesar, son of the divine Caesar, consul for the seventh time).*

© *British Museum*

into Ethiopia, and reach relative safety. In the meantime, Antony tried to prevent Cornelius Gallus from attacking Egypt from the west. He took a squadron of ships and some infantry to meet Gallus but was defeated and lost the ships. In the west, Cleopatra's general Seleucus half-heartedly defended Pelusium, but gave up and let Octavian's troops pass by unopposed. Antony rallied, took some cavalry to clash with Octavian's advance guard, which he routed, and sent them fleeing back to the main army. He returned to Alexandria flushed with success, celebrating his victory in the old style.

But it was all desperate bravado. Antony knew when he was beaten. Allegedly he challenged Octavian to single combat, and received the supercilious reply that he could find better ways to end his life. The main battle was to take place next day, on the first day of the month Sextilis, later renamed August, in honour of Augustus. Antony told his friends the night before the battle was fought that he could not hope to win, and was merely looking for an honourable death. That same night, haunting music was heard in the streets of Alexandria, together with the noise of a procession of unseen people leaving the city by the eastern gate — the god Dionysus and his revellers deserting Antony, before he finally fell.

The next morning the army on the high ground at the Canopus gate watched the fleet sail out to engage Octavian's ships, but they put up no fight.

There was probably a prearranged signal, or perhaps some quick-thinking captains copied each other in quick succession, as Antony's crews put up their oars and waited. Then the two fleets became one fleet as Antony's ships sailed towards Octavian's and joined them. The soldiers had perhaps expected something of the sort, and may even have known that it was going to happen. There was no reason why they should sacrifice themselves for a defeated man. It was much better to go over to Octavian now, and perhaps obtain good terms from him. The cavalry rode off with their swords sheathed. The legionaries fought desultorily for a while, then surrendered or ran away.

Antony rode back to Alexandria, wondering if Cleopatra had betrayed him. She had retired to her mausoleum and barricaded the door, so, when Antony was told that she was already dead, he had no real reason to doubt the story. He asked his slave Eros to kill him, but Eros killed himself instead, so Antony tried to stab himself with his sword. Even a quick death deserted Antony, for he only succeeded in wounding himself painfully. When he had revived sufficiently for Cleopatra's slaves to communicate with him, he learned that she was not dead after all, so he had himself carried on a litter to her tomb, where she and her two servants Iras and Charmian hauled him up to the level of the window and dragged the litter inside. The romantic death in Cleopatra's arms is probably true. Even if it could be proved beyond all doubt that it never happened that way, no-one would be convinced, because the scenario is part of western tradition. How and why the central characters arrived at this desperate point can be reinterpreted, amended, debated and disputed, but once they *had* arrived at that point, history shades off into legend, and that is always more enduring than mere prosaic fact.

9 Posterity

Cleopatra survived for a few more days after Antony's death. Octavian negotiated with her, and both Plutarch and Dio say that he went to see her in her mausoleum, but there is probably no truth in the story, which was doubtless invented. The ancient authors often used to depict such scenes in order to disseminate political and historical ideas of their own through the mouths of their main characters. It is also said that Octavian wanted to preserve Cleopatra alive for his triumph in Rome, but that too is probably make-believe. It was much tidier to take over Egypt with all contenders for its throne safely and quite unequivocally removed. The sympathies of the Egyptian people for their Queen might cause problems if she were allowed to survive, and those sympathies could also extend to her children. Caesarion was sought after and killed, because he represented a double threat to Octavian, in that he was both heir to the Egyptian throne, and had been recognised as Caesar's son. His fate was a foregone conclusion. Antyllus, who was only 14 years old, was dragged out of hiding in the unfinished temple dedicated to his father Antony, and killed on the spot. There were three other children, but Octavian spared them. Alexander Helios, Cleopatra Selene, and Ptolemy Philadelphus were sent to Rome. Eventually Cleopatra Selene was married to king Juba and lived out the rest of her life in North Africa. The two boys may have gone with her, or they may have remained in Rome, keeping a low profile. Their ultimate fates are unknown, but lack of knowledge about them need not denote their early demise. They may have grown up in the household of Octavia, who was famed for her care of all Antony's surviving children. Iullus Antonius, Antony's second son by Fulvia, had a promising career, being married to Marcella, Octavia's daughter by her first husband. He was consul in 10, and went on to govern the province of Asia from 7 to 6. Unfortunately he was implicated in the scandalous affair of 2 BC when Augustus' daughter Julia was accused of adultery with several eminent men, and exiled. Iullus Antonius was executed.

Antony's two daughters by Octavia carried on the line via their marriages, the elder sister to Lucius, the son of Domitius Ahenobarbus, and the younger to Tiberius' brother Drusus. Through them, three Emperors of Rome could claim descent from Antony. Two of them, Caligula and Nero, were not the creditable descendants that he could have wished for, but Claudius inherited his grandfather Antony's talents for sensible administration, and his regard for humanity and humane treatment of those whom he considered deserving. Claudius could be cruel, like Antony, but also like Antony, he tried to be fair and just, and could be very generous. Antony would have approved of him.

Cleopatra died most likely, according to the traditional story, by the bite of the poisonous asp, which may have been arranged by or in consultation with Octavian. The legend has it that as soon as he heard of her death he sent for the *psylli* who were trained to suck out the poison of snake bites and, as more than one author has pointed out, it was very strange that Octavian should send for them if Cleopatra's death was supposed to have taken him by surprise. Some scholars have surmised that Octavian allowed Cleopatra to choose her own way of death because it relieved him of the necessity of executing her, and others have highlighted the religious connections between the asp and the divinity that its bite was supposed to bestow. In death, Cleopatra outdid anything that the Romans could have dreamed up for her. She was dressed in all her finery and wore her crown, which her devoted servants carefully arranged just before they too died with her. The whole scene is quite credible for a Queen who knew how important it was to cultivate and maintain an image.

Octavian honoured the last wishes of both Antony and Cleopatra and buried them side by side. Their tomb has never been found. Immediately afterwards, Octavian took over Egypt as his own preserve. He installed as governor the general Cornelius Gallus, who had attacked from the west in coordination with Octavian's advance from the east. Gallus was not a senator, but a member of the middle classes, the equites. Such an elevated command for an equestrian was an innovation, perhaps a hasty measure adopted because Gallus was on the spot and Octavian needed a suitable governor very quickly. If such it was, it became a regular equestrian post, one of the most sought after rewards of the equestrian career. Octavian-Augustus never readjusted the position of the governor of Egypt, nor the relationship of the province to himself. No senator was allowed to enter the country except by special dispensation from himself, and later Emperors saw no reason to relax this vigilance. Much of Rome's corn supply came from Egypt, and its wealth enabled Augustus to maintain his position in Rome, discharging his debts and paying all the promised donatives to his supporters and troops.

He could afford to be generous to the memory of Cleopatra, after having deliberately fomented war against her. The statue that Caesar had placed in the temple of Venus was allowed to remain there, and an Egyptian official, Cleopatra's friend Archibius, paid 1000 talents to Octavian to save most of the other statues and portraits of her. Antony did not fare so well. The news of his

28   *The statue of Augustus from Prima Porta, Italy, now in the Vatican Museum.*
      The scenes depicted on the breastplate celebrate the return of the Roman standards
      from Parthia, achieved by diplomatic means rather than by warfare. Augustus
      brought to a close the campaigns begun by Crassus, and continued by Antony.

Photo Karen Dixon

death was read out in the Senate by Cicero's son Marcus. It cannot have been merely a fortuitous choice of reader; the irony is obvious to say the least. The Senate declared Antony's birthday *nefastus*, and decreed that all statues, busts and portraits should be destroyed. The few items which remain may perhaps have been oversights, or they may even be wrongly identified. Only the coin portraits can legitimately claim to be unequivocal representations of Antony. His name was to be erased from all monuments all over the Roman world, and in their zeal to comply, some provincials chiselled out the name Antonius wherever it seemed to be connected to the name Marcus, perhaps because Octavian had decided that such thoroughness was only right and proper. Thus Antony's memory was damned for ever, and the world was instructed to forget about him. The world, however, did not comply. Some of the details are lost, but Mark Antony has never been forgotten.

Bibliography

A Note on the Ancient Sources

There is no contemporary account of Antony's life. When he joined Caesar in Gaul, some of Antony's exploits were deemed worthy of inclusion in the *Commentaries*, better known to us as Caesar's *Gallic War*. Thereafter, the only surviving contemporary information concerning Antony is embodied in the letters and speeches of Cicero, none of which were favourable to Antony, but the letters provide an unparalleled account of the political and social developments in Rome, while the speeches allow an insight into the turbulent war-mongering against Antony. Some correspondence from Antony has been preserved, for instance, the letter which he sent from northern Italy is quoted and shredded paragraph by paragraph in the *Philippics*, and his communications with Cicero are repeated, ostensibly verbatim, in Cicero's letters to Atticus.

The history of the Triumvirate will never be entirely recovered, not least because the last of the Triumvirs, Octavian, was not particularly interested in preserving the information for posterity. From 44 onwards, the historical record for a reconstruction of a life of Antony is fraught with difficulties, because the facts were distorted, or in some cases suppressed, to suit the tastes of Augustus, who rewrote his own part in the civil wars, and presented Antony as the sinister and dangerous enemy of Rome, under the influence of Cleopatra.

Later authors used works that are now lost to us or known only in fragments. These include Plutarch, who wrote during the second half of the first century, and the second-century historian Appian, whose work has survived only in part; only 11 of his original 24 books are extant. His history of the civil wars beyond 35, when Sextus Pompey was executed, has been lost. Neither of them are entirely hostile to Antony, but the truth of what they recorded is sometimes dubious. Plutarch in particular was influenced by the experiences of his grandfather, who was forced to take part in a convoy, carrying supplies by hand to Antony's camp at Actium, when the encirclement by Octavian and Agrippa cut the Antonians off from easier sources of supply.

The history of Rome written by Titus Livius, known as Livy, fails us for the period of Antony's life. Some fragments survive from the later copyists, and perhaps much of his work is preserved in Dio's Roman history, who wrote in the early third century. By then, the depiction of Antony as debauched, irresponsible, incompetent and most of all as a failure was indelible, so any departure from this theme depended upon personal opinion.

Modern scholars are assisted by the archaeological and numismatic evidence that has accumulated over the centuries between Antony's demise and the present day. Although the Senate decreed that his memory was to be eternally damned, and his portraits were to be destroyed, nothing could be done to eradictae the coinage, which has much to tell us about the political history and the self-promotion of the great men of the day. The coin portraits are not totally accurate, but can still reveal something of the character of the main participants in the civil wars and political upheavals in the second half of the first century BC.

Further Reading

There is an impressive collection of ancient and modern literature covering the period of Antony's life. This list includes the main sources, in which more detailed bibliographies can be found if readers wish to take the subject further.

Ancient sources

The following works are all available in the Loeb Classical Library. Each volume gives the Latin or Greek text together with a parallel English translation.

Appian	*Roman History* (vols. 2 to 4)
Caesar	*Gallic War*
Caesar	*Civil Wars*
Cicero	*Letters to Atticus* (3 vols)
	Letters to His Friends (3 vols)
	Philippics
Dio	*Roman History* (vols. 3 to 6)
Plutarch	*Life of Antony*

Modern Works

Cambridge Ancient History Vol. IX *The Roman Republic 133 - 44 BC* edited by SA Cook et al. Cambridge University Press 1932

Cambridge Ancient History Vol. X *The Augustan Empire, 43 BC - AD 69* edited by A K Bowman et al. Cambridge University Press 2nd ed 1997 (The first edition published in 1934 is still useful)

Carter, J M   *The Battle of Actium.* Hamish Hamilton 1970

Flamarion, E   *Cleopatra: from history to legend.* Thames and Hudson 1997

Grant, M   *Cleopatra.* Weidenfeld and Nicolson 1972

Grant, M   *Roman History from Coins.* Cambridge University Press 1968

Gruen, E S   *The Last Generation of the Roman Republic.* University of California Press 1974, reprinted in paperback 1995

Lindsay, J   *Cleopatra.* Constable 1971

Lindsay, J   *Mark Antony and his Contemporaries.* London 1936

Meier, C   *Caesar.* Harper Collins 1995

Richardson, G W   Actium *Journal of Roman Studies* 27, 1937, 153-64

Roberts, A   *Mark Antony: his life and times.* Malvern Publishing Company 1988

Syme, R   *The Roman Revolution.* Oxford University Press 1939

Tarn, W W   The Battle of Actium *Journal of Roman Studies* 21, 1931, 173-99

Tarn, W W   Antony's legions *Classical Quarterly* 1932, 75 -89

Weigall, A   *Mark Antony: his life and times.* London 1931

Index

A note on Roman personal names: in the text and in the index the main characters are listed under their Anglicised names, e.g.: Antony, Pompey, etc., while the rest are indexed under their family names, e.g.: Bibulus is entered under Calpurnius Bibulus; Catilina is under Sergius Catilina. The name Octavian is not strictly accurate until after the adoption of Octavius by Julius Caesar, but for simplicity this name is used throughout. Octavian did not become Augustus until after Antony's death. In this index, references to Antony and Octavian are abbreviated to A. and O.